Ireland's Forgotten Past

IRELAND

Ballycastle
Coleraine
Derry
Antrim
Donegal
ULSTER
Enniskillen
Belfast
Downpatrick
Armagh
Monaghan
Sligo
Cavan
Castlebar
Dundalk
CONNACHT
Navan
Drogheda
Athlone
Galway
LEINSTER
Dublin
Naas
Carlow
Kilkenny
Limerick
Wexford
Tralee
Waterford
Dingle
MUNSTER
Cork

N
W E
S

Turtle Bunbury

Ireland's Forgotten Past

A History of the Overlooked & Disremembered

Thames & Hudson

Contents

'The past is never where you think you left it.'

Katherine Anne Porter

Introduction

The first inkling of humanity in Ireland involves the butchering of a bear near the River Shannon almost 13,000 years ago. Following the maxim of thirty generations every thousand years, that brings us back a mind-numbing 390 generations. The first Bunbury arrived in Ireland a mere eleven generations ago, either on the run or on the make, depending on your perspective. He settled amid the healthy pastures of County Carlow in the 1660s and bought a farm for his son – the farm where I grew up and where my two young daughters are now enjoying their childhood.

Part of my fascination with the past stems from being raised in a Victorian country house stuffed with family portraits, musty books and bizarre curiosities scooped up by ancestors on their travels. Certainly, a number of the stories that follow were born from a desire to understand Ireland as it was for my poker-faced forebears.

I am also in love with the landscape around me. I live within a three-minute hop of an overgrown ringfort that was once home to perhaps seven or eight families. In the field beside it, a sound-less underground stream flows east for half a mile before tumbling into a river alongside the very last traces of a monastery so old that almost nothing is known of it. Just south of the monastery is a fabulous dolmen, a portal tomb constructed by unknown, unknowable Neolithic hands some five thousand years ago. We cannot quite see the dolmen from our home but we can see the long golden strip of the barley field that runs behind it, a strip that transpired to be stuffed with ancient barrows and circular enclosures when a friendly drone zeroed in on it from the skies above during the long, hot summer of 2018. Up until that time, nobody had any idea that the barley field had a past.

'What's past is prologue,' observes Shakespeare's Antonio in *The Tempest*, and yet sometimes the prologue is indecipherable or nowhere to be seen. The dolmen earns a brief mention in the occasional tourist brochure but I have never seen any record of the monastery or ringfort – no archived memories of who built them, who dwelt there, who slept, ate, thought, laughed, loved, mourned or died there. It is simply the shapes of earth and stone that reveal the human touch.

The same can be said for so much of Ireland. Every field, hill, stream and rock seems to hold another secret about the island's past, even as we glide by indifferent or unaware: hilltop summits crowned with ancient forts, rocky cairns and the ghostly outlines of primeval forests; riversides studded with ruined castles, hollow mills and crumbling farmsteads; the bramble-strewn shells of abandoned canals and copper mines; the stumps of pillars that once carried railway lines; the overgrown graveyards where the forgotten bloodlines lie.

Forgotten: 'for', meaning 'away'; 'gotten' from a Germanic verb 'to grasp' – hence, something that has got away, the grasp of a memory. What was once remembered and acknowledged has become neglected, overlooked, disregarded and unremembered, perhaps irretrievably so.

The vast majority of this world's occurrences have simply faded into oblivion. It was not until the eruption of the Information Age in the past half-century that attempts to chronicle the past became in any way mainstream. A change is coming now. The appetite to reconstruct the fragmented world of our forebears is an increasingly powerful market force, supported by big business interests in genealogy, tourism, the movie industry and such like. The challenge will be to keep track of what truths are told, to understand the motives of the storyteller, to ensure those facts are verifiable, that the spin can be balanced and counterbalanced, that the reshaping of the past does not imperil the future.

This book shines a light on thirty-six lesser-known tales from the annals of Irish history. Some have been snubbed for reasons unclear. Others are simply so odd that it's high time they came to light again. The cast includes a pair of ill-fated prehistoric chieftains, a psychopathic Viking monarch, a chivalrous Norman warrior, a dazzling English traitor, an ingenious tailor, an outstanding warhorse, a fanatical spymaster, a brothel queen, a randy prince and an insanely prolific sculptor.

It begins with a volcano and concludes with Operation Shamrock, a humanitarian mission at the close of the Second World War that not only showcased the innate Irish empathy for the downtrodden but also heralded a brave new Ireland, a country that would ultimately go on to become not simply an outlying frontier of European eccentricity but a remarkable global hub that, in the present century, consistently punches way above its weight.

Although the tales are not specifically linked, I am of the view that almost everything is connected, one way or another, when one digs deep enough. Taken as a whole, these stories underline why Ireland is such an exceptional island for anyone interested in the past. There is an awful lot of amazing history out there – the juiciest plots, the greatest twists, the richest characters – and yet so much of it remains, even now, forgotten.

Turtle Bunbury
County Carlow

1 Of Tetrapods & Volcanic Rings

 Should you ever find yourself on Valentia Island off the coast of County Kerry, you might venture to its northern shore in pursuit of a fossilized trackway, unwittingly imprinted for eternity by a Devonian tetrapod that pitter-pattered upon this planet 385 million years ago. The footprints of that 1-m (3¼-ft)-long creature are among the oldest fossils in Ireland but just in case you think this four-legged beauty sounds like a dinosaur, please observe that it lived 150 million years *before* the dinosaurs.

Fast forward to about 66 million years ago when a giant asteroid, perhaps 15 km (9 miles) in diameter, slammed into the Earth and wiped out approximately three-quarters of the known animal and plant kingdom, including all non-avian dinosaurs. That astral cataclysm spelled the end of what's called the Cretaceous period and the start of the Palaeogene period, at which point Ireland was hovering on a latitude roughly equivalent to where Portugal sits today. As such, the island was in pole position for the considerable turbulence that befell the world when, five million years into the Palaeogene, the North Atlantic Ocean was born.

The ocean's birth was a long-drawn-out affair. In Ireland, it was marked by the eruption of the Antrim basalts (which created the Giant's Causeway) and a swell of scorching hot magma gushing across the Mountains of Mourne. Its legacy can clearly be seen at the Ring of Gullion in County Armagh, through which enormous numbers of people drive on the Dublin to Belfast road every day. The ring measures 11 km (7 miles) in diameter and covers more than 15,000 hectares (37,000 acres). Its huge rocks are the remnants of a massive volcanic caldera that collapsed, as calderas are wont to do. Simultaneously, layer upon layer of magma intruded into the heart of the volcano itself to form

Slieve Gullion (576 m/1,890 ft), now the highest peak in County Armagh.

Attempts to grapple with all this shape-shifting geology are complicated by the miscellaneous glaciers that left their mark during the ensuing Ice Age; numerous glaciations eroded the region's weaker sediments, leaving the hard volcanic rocks of the Ring of Gullion and Slieve Gullion standing sturdy and proud. A geological fault running through the low ground between the ring and the north of Slieve Gullion became a glacial ribbon lake, now known as Cam Lough.

In the Celtic legends, the warrior Fionn mac Cumhaill is tricked into diving into another of Slieve Gullion's lakes by the Cailleach Bhéara (the Hag of Beara); the moment his muscular torso hits the water, he is transformed into a weak and withered

old man. At length, he guzzles an antidote and is restored to full strength but his hair remains white ever after. Such fabulous tales gather added kudos when one visits the five-thousand-year-old passage tomb near the Hag's Lake; aligned with the setting sun on the winter solstice, this is the highest such tomb in Ireland.

And just in case you're starting to think five thousand years is a very long time ago, it is, in fact, only 0.001 per cent of the 385 million years that have passed since that Valentia tetrapod took a stroll.

2 It Starts with a Bear

Somewhere in the region of 12,800 years ago, a hunter in County Clare confronted a big brown bear with a sharp stone flint. Having won the battle, the hunter dragged the bear into a cave near present-day Ennis where he or she began butchering the beast, stripping the meat and smashing the bones to access its high-protein marrow. At least, that's one conceivable explanation for a surviving bear patella – or kneecap – found in the aforesaid cave. A series of lopsided, man-made cuts on that patella are presently regarded as the earliest conclusive evidence of mankind in Ireland.

The Palaeolithic bear hunter must have been among the first humans to take advantage of the melting waters that freed up the lands of northern Europe after an Ice Age that had lasted nearly 100,000 years. The rising sea levels created the island of Ireland as a separate entity to Britain and the rest of western Europe.

Nearly three thousand winters after the death of the bear, a band of humans made a clearing in a primitive forest between

Creadan Head and Dunmore East in County Waterford. They constructed what is believed to be the oldest settlement in Ireland; thousands of stone knives, scrapers and tiny blades made from chert pebbles have been found at the site. At about this time, similar settlements sprang up at Ballyferriter, near Dingle, County Kerry, and at Mount Sandel, near Coleraine, County Derry.

Our knowledge of what Ireland was like during the Mesolithic period remains profoundly vague. These people were shorter than us, and shorter-lived, too, with lifespans perhaps half the length of our own. They may have been dark-skinned and blue-eyed, like England's ten-thousand-year-old Cheddar Man is thought to have been. They would have spoken their own fully-fledged language, incomprehensible to modern ears. Excavations at Mount Sandel suggest they lived in egg-shaped, dome-roofed structures, con-structed of timber posts, saplings, hide, bark, thatch and reeds. Perhaps a dozen people could comfortably fit into each hut; the inhabitants snoozed around a central hearth that afforded them a holy trinity of heat, light and a place to cook. The flint-smith was of pivotal importance, crafting arrowheads, hide scrapers and spears with razor-sharp blades, as well as polished stone picks and axes.

Women played a key role in the quest for food. During the summer, these plucky souls foraged for crab apples, lily seeds, berries and protein-rich hazelnuts that could be kept in storage for the leaner months. Taking to the water in dug-out log canoes, they trapped and speared the migrating salmon, sea bass, plaice, flounder and autumnal eel that swam in and around the estuaries and coastline; the fish were smoked or dried on wooden racks just beside their huts.

In the cold, wet winters, Mesolithic people fed on wild pigs, hares and other edible animals, as well as birds such as wood pigeon, teal and mallard. Eagle bones found at Mount Sandel

are thought to indicate a fashionable fancy for eagle feathers in clothing and headdresses rather than a passion for eagle meat; traces of red ochre on flint blades suggest that they also liked to paint their bodies in times of ceremony.

There were other Mesolithic communities in Ireland, primarily along the coast of northern Ulster, as well as the Blackwater Valley in the south. Still more people settled on the shores of Galway Bay, where they evidently had a soft spot for limpets. Ireland's oldest-known graveyard is a Mesolithic burial pit near the River Shannon at Hermitage, County Limerick, where the efficient cremation of two bodies perhaps 9,500 years ago indicates that the funeral party were no strangers to such procedures.

It is no surprise that the population stuck to the coast and rivers, given that the interior of Ireland at this time was effectively an impenetrable forest; a squirrel could apparently swing from tree to tree from Malin Head, on the northernmost coast of County Donegal, all the way down to Mizen Head on the southernmost tip of County Cork, without ever touching the ground. That said, some hunters made it inland as far as Boora Bog in County Offaly where there is yet more archaeological evidence of humans chopping up animals and fish with axes and flint nine millennia ago.

Life in Mesolithic Ireland appears to have continued undisturbed, generation after generation, for several thousand years. Our knowledge of this epoch of early humanity in Ireland is wreathed in emptiness and speculation. Estimates of the island's peak population vary from 3,000 to as high as 40,000. In any event, the age was to come to an end with the arrival of the first Neolithic settlers almost six thousand years ago. The fate of the Mesolithic inhabitants is unclear but they were almost certainly either displaced or assimilated by the highly driven and intriguing newcomers.

3 Neolithic Stargazers

Just outside the town of Carlow stands a work of immense human ingenuity and antiquity. Known as the Brownshill Dolmen, this burial tomb comprises two hefty, sculpted boulders standing upright, atop of which tilts a massive, weather-beaten granite slab that is estimated to weigh a whopping 103 tonnes: that's about the same as seventeen fully grown Indian elephants or a Boeing 757 jet. If the All Blacks and the Lions rugby teams were to unite with the hundred strongest National Football League players from the USA, they would struggle to nudge the Brownshill capstone by an inch. How they managed to elevate that formidable slab remains a mystery but archaeologists believe that Brownshill and the other 180 or so portal tombs in Ireland were probably created by a combination of beefy humans and brawny oxen, working with timber sledges greased with lard or tallow, as well as rolling trunks, earth ramps, knotted ropes, levers, counterweights and pivots.

Although the site has not yet been excavated, the Brownshill Dolmen is thought to have been created in about 3900 BC. Dolmens are a type of megalith (from the Greek for 'large stones'), of which at least fifteen hundred were constructed across Ireland during what is known as the Neolithic period. Limited excavations carried out to date have yielded human bones, both burnt and unsullied, as well as decorated pottery, beads, bone pins and flints. These were clearly burial tombs built by a people who cremated and then venerated their dead.

In 2019, scientists published their findings after a genetic analysis of teeth belonging to eleven individuals found in two tombs at Carrowmore, Ireland's oldest Neolithic complex, on the Cúil Irra peninsula in County Sligo. The results revealed that

those buried within were from the same family and predominantly male, and that the tombs may have been used for at least twelve generations.

While some megaliths clearly served as family mausoleums, many were also brilliantly designed with one eye on solar or lunar events taking place in the skies above. In other words, they doubled up as the world's first clocks – elaborate sundials that enabled these budding farmers to keep track of time. Some were aligned with the spring equinox, the start of the sowing season, or the autumnal equinox, when the harvest is traditionally complete. Yet more were designed to show the halfway point between solstices and equinoxes, providing the four cross-quarter days of Imbolg (February), Beltane (May), Lughnasa (August) and

Samhain (November), while others appear to be attuned to the eight-year cycle of Venus or to the three stars of Orion's Belt, one of the principal indicators of the solstices. Some were modestly harmonized to reflect relationships with other sacred monuments or natural topographical features in the vicinity.

The Neolithic *pièce de résistance* is at Newgrange in County Meath where an astounding underground burial chamber is tucked inside a man-made mound of 200,000 tonnes of earth and loose stones. Every 21 December, or winter solstice, the rising sun shoots its rays down an 18.8-m (61¾-ft)-long, damp-proofed passageway into a chamber where it triumphantly strikes a triple-spiral motif on the back wall, illuminating the entire space for the next fourteen minutes. Cloudy mornings aside, it has achieved this feat without fail for approximately 5,200 solstices in a row.

As well as megaliths, there are at least 187 surviving stone circles in Ireland, although untold numbers have been destroyed over the past millennia. For instance, the thirty monuments that stand at Carrowmore today represent less than half the number counted in a survey of the area in 1837. Not all of these stone circles were constructed in the Neolithic period, some hail from the Bronze Age. Although their purpose appears to have been primarily ceremonial or funerary, the monuments often indicate a keen astronomical awareness. Others are reputedly aligned with ley lines, the mysterious energy channels that are said to criss-cross the globe.

The architects of these cosmological masterpieces arrived from afar early in the 4th millennium BC and dominated much of the Irish landscape until their disappearance shortly before 2000 BC. Sadly, we know precious little about them save that they were skilled farmers with a profound knowledge of astronomy and engineering, as well as a deep commitment to the afterlife. They are thought to have come from Galicia in Spain or from Brittany in France; both landscapes are also liberally spotted with megaliths. They were predominantly olive-skinned and dark-haired, not unlike present-day Sardinians, and lived in huts constructed with timber beams, finely woven wood (wattle) and dried mud (daub).

You would not want to pick a fight with someone from the Neolithic Age. A scientific analysis of arm bones belonging to Neolithic women from central Europe indicated that they were between 11 and 16 per cent more muscular than Cambridge University's female rowing crews. These women came of age in the wake of an agricultural revolution that began in places such as the Fertile Crescent of the Middle East ten thousand years ago and gradually inched its way across Europe.

The Neolithic people who populated Ireland had acquired much of the knowledge of the Mesopotamian farmers, including such energy-saving innovations as using pack animals to carry cumbersome weights. They also knew how to mine for porcellanite, a china-like stone much tougher than flint, which proved ideal for axes, sickles and digging implements. Over 18,000 axes from this period have been found in Ireland to date; the best examples are always made of porcellanite mined on either Rathlin Island, off the coast of County Antrim, or near Cushendall in the Glens of Antrim.

With fire, beast and porcellanite axe, Neolithic people cleared the upland forests, converted the land into extensive fields and cultivated barley and emmer wheat. Elsewhere they farmed indigenous pigs on the grassy pastures, as well as cattle, goats and sheep that they somehow shipped into Ireland. Beneath a raised blanket bog on the cliff edge of northern County Mayo, a series of stone walls mark the outline of the Céide Fields, an efficiently planned 1,200-hectare (3,000-acre) dairy farm that may have been operational as far back as 3000 BC.

Neolithic people were also no amateurs when it came to boatbuilding. In 1901 a perfectly preserved log boat was found at the Lurgan bog in County Galway. Measuring over 14 m (45 ft) long and 1 m (3¼ ft) wide, it was hollowed out of a single oak trunk four thousand years ago by a people armed with nothing more than stone tools and fire. Archaeologists believe it may have been a ceremonial boat and that it would have required at least twelve oarsmen. A number of other sleek Neolithic dug-out canoes have been found since, including the 12-m (40-ft)-long Annaghkeen canoe in Lough Corrib, County Galway, which was carbon-dated to 2500 BC, and the remains of an oak-wood log boat at Oldbridge on the River Boyne, carbon-dated to between 3300 BC and 2900 BC.

There is certainly much to learn. Following the summer drought of 2018, archaeologists found almost forty hitherto unnoticed monuments in Brú na Bóinne, a part of the Boyne Valley that was already home to the world's largest concentration of Neolithic henges as well as its greatest wealth of megalithic art. Among the new discoveries were another monument aligned with sunrise on the winter solstice, two circular henges (one 150 m (492 ft) in diameter), and the remnants of a massive avenue made from large tree trunks. Another large passage tomb was discovered at Dowth Hall in County Meath in 2018.

The Neolithic Age came to a relatively abrupt halt in about 2400 BC when Ireland's population plunged by a whopping 90 per cent, precipitating the widespread abandonment and destruction of their settlements. Some have proposed this was caused by a bacterial plague, akin to the Black Death of the 1340s, but there is mounting evidence to suggest that the Neolithic inhabitants of Ireland were victims of a mass genocide. Their demise also appears to have coincided with the arrival of a new people from afar, heralding the onset of the Bell Beaker culture and the Bronze Age.

4 The Bell Beakers

 Although they might sound like a nice family from Gloucestershire, the Bell Beakers were actually a vast group of people who followed a way of life that predominated across maritime Europe about four thousand years ago. As well as having their own set of religious beliefs and languages, the Bell Beaker folk advocated a material culture characterized by a remarkable ability to work with copper, bronze and gold, as well as a fondness for good beer. This mindset is thought to have originated along the Tagus estuary in present-day Portugal, with strong flavours of North Africa added to the mix. The name 'Bell Beaker' derives from the decorated, bell-shaped beakers, or clay vessels, that its adherents used to drink and eat from, as well as to smelt copper ore and carry the ashes of their dead.

The general belief is that Ireland's first Bell Beaker folk arrived from Portugal in about 2400 BC, having sailed up the Atlantic in pursuit of copper and other riches. Their most

successful port of call was at Ross Island in County Kerry, where these metallurgical wizards began mining arsenical copper. They had deduced that axes and knives made of copper were much more effective and durable than those made of stone. As such, they dug lateral tunnels using a combination of fire and antler picks, shovelling out the copper ore with bones shaped from the shoulders of cattle.

Judging by the different types of pottery found across Ireland, the country seems to have contained many distinctive Bell Beaker communities. They also differed from their contemporaries in England and Wales and yet, perhaps inevitably, they had much in common with their Neolithic predecessors. They certainly adapted to the pastoral way of life and extended existing communal burial sites like Newgrange and the Beltany Stone Circle in County Donegal, just as they did with the Neolithic graves at Stonehenge in England.

However, a marked reduction in migration over the ensuing centuries may have left the newcomers isolated. They became more clan-like, developing social hierarchies, warring among themselves and building defensive forts on hilltops. They found it expedient to invent the bronze halberd, a lethal broad blade mounted on a 1-m (3¼-ft)-long pole; with its formidable thrusting power, the weapon would soon become a prized possession for warriors throughout Europe. Stone wristguards used by archers in the Bell Beaker period have also been found in abundance across Ireland.

The admiration for megaliths went into decline. Passage tombs were abandoned and blocked up; parts of the Great Mound at Knowth in the Boyne Valley, aligned to both equinoxes, were destroyed. Perhaps the deterioration of the Irish weather affected the zest for astronomy; the warm, dry climate that the Neolithic people had enjoyed became decidedly damper during the ensuing millennia.

Cremation continued to be popular but there was some geographical divergence in terms of burial practice. Along the Atlantic coast, simple wedge tombs were favoured, while in the north and east there was a tendency towards individual barrows (or tumuli) and cist graves, sometimes topped with cairns. The dead were often given a 'crouched burial', with their legs folded up to their chest. Many were buried alongside pottery vessels and weapons, particularly copper daggers.

As well as taking immense pride in the quality and beauty of their vessels, the Bell Beaker people were champions of the *fulacht fiadh*, the horse-shaped troughs in which they cooked. By continually adding piping hot rocks into these pits, water could be brought to the boil in less than thirty minutes. Once the boil was on, a few more hot rocks kept the water simmering. In 1952, working to the Victorian housekeeper's time-honoured recipe of twenty minutes to the pound (450 g) and twenty minutes over, Professor Michael O'Kelly cooked a straw-wrapped 4.5-kg (10-lb) leg of mutton to perfection. There is an intriguing belief that *fulacht fiadh* were also used to make a palatable home-brew ale by immersing hot stones in a wooden mash.

By 2200 BC, the pioneering Ross Island copper mine had been joined by the massive Mount Gabriel mine in West Cork, where twenty-five mineshafts were cut into a hill near Schull. Fires were lit against the face of each shaft; pots of water were then hurled on the scorched rock, causing it to shatter, before the labourers advanced with cobble scoops and stone hammers to draw the copper out. Smaller-scale mines operated at places like Bunmahon in County Waterford, Allihies on the Beara Peninsula in County Cork and Avoca in County Wicklow. By this means, an estimated 370 tonnes of finished copper were produced in Irish mines over the next three centuries; plentiful traces of Irish copper have been identified in contemporary artefacts found in Britain, the Netherlands and Brittany.

Copper axes certainly proved useful when it came to clearing Ireland's lowland forests to provide fresh pastures for Bell Beaker livestock. On hand to help was a new four-legged species they brought to Ireland: the horse. Although by no means numerous, these small, willowy creatures were primarily used for work and transport. Horsehair was also useful for insulation and bedding, while sometimes a hungry belly dictated that these hardy beasts were chopped up for the *fulacht fiadh*.

The construction of the Mount Gabriel copper mine coincided with a growing awareness that tin turns copper into bronze, a malleable yet even stronger metal. Not only did this prompt the start of the Bronze Age in Ireland, but it also inspired considerable trade with the tin panners of Cornwall, Devon and Brittany. In return, ever-sturdier axes, daggers, halberds and wristguards made their way eastwards from Ireland. The Bell Beaker people also had an intricate understanding of gold. Although not a particularly taxing process, they had enough experience of goldwork to know how to identify the ore to begin with. They also understood the innovative techniques required to recover gold and convert it into desirable objects.

Gold has been an obsession of Ireland's elite for a very long time. More Bronze Age gold hoards have been found in Ireland than anywhere else on Earth, including eighty gold lunulae, the must-have trinket of the late 3rd millennium BC. These decorated neck collars, shaped like a crescent moon, are made of thin, hammered sheets of gold. Consequently, the National Museum of Ireland's collection of Bronze Age goldwork is one of the largest in the world, and still growing. In 2018, a farmer found four solid-gold wristbands while digging a drain near the Derry–Donegal border, less than 8 km (5 miles) from the Beltany Stone Circle. The earliest gold objects in the National Museum's collection were made in about 2200 BC. A hoard of ornaments found at Gorteenreagh in County Clare yielded a gold hair fastener (lock-ring) of almost inconceivable intricacy, decorated in minute concentric wires, no more than a third of a millimetre thick. The source of gold used to make all this Bronze Age bling is something of an enigma. Some was imported from Cornwall, perhaps by the same people who traded tin, and some undoubtedly came from Iberia, Portugal and further afield. However, the vast majority of these glittering sun discs and lunulae were made of pure Irish gold.

It may have washed from the Goldmines River and other rivers that flow off the igneous rocks of the Wicklow Mountains, or from the rugged slopes of Croagh Patrick in County Mayo, said to be the source of the gold found in the torcs (neck-rings), crowns and bracelets of the ancient royal families of Ireland. Implements for melting and casting gold have been found in the Bog of Cullen, on the Tipperary–Limerick border, along with gold ornaments. Gold used in cloak and sleeve fasteners has been traced to places such as the Inishowen Peninsula of County Donegal and the Sperrin Mountains of County Tyrone. The gravelly beds of the rivers and streams that criss-cross the Mountains of Mourne provided the gold found in an outstanding collection of 146 collars, neck-rings, bracelets, dress fastenings and other decorative objects found at Mooghaun in County Clare. Regarded as the largest gold hoard found outside the eastern Mediterranean, it was unearthed near a hillfort that was of considerable ritualistic importance in the late Bronze Age.

The Bell Beaker culture began to fade from about 1700 BC, eight centuries after it first reached Ireland. The copper mines limped on for a while but the industrial legacy of the age also continued at places such as Rathgall in south County Wicklow, where, in about 900 BC, the 7-hectare (18-acre) hillfort appears to have been home to a substantial workshop for manufacturing exotic glass beads of translucent turquoise, as well as bracelets of jet and lignite, and other objects of amber, gold and stone.

The passion for gold also survived. In the 12th-century Book of Leinster, the men of Leinster were described as 'Lagenians of the Gold' on account of all the gold in their kingdom. According to the *Lebor Gabála Érenn* (The Book of the Taking of Ireland), a poetic history penned by Christian monks in the 11th century, Ireland's first gold mine was established on the banks of the River Liffey by King Tigernmas, a Milesian king, whose seventy-seven-year reign is said to have been contemporaneous with those of kings David and Solomon of Israel (*c.* 990–930 BC). This also coincided with the late Bronze Age, by which time Ireland had become something of a European hub for goldworking. New techniques for twisting bars and strips saw a dramatic increase in both the quality and quantity of gold objects in Ireland; such items have reputedly been found as far away as Egypt.

The late Bronze Age also saw a craze for elaborately decorated torcs as status symbols; a gold torc found at Clonmacnoise, County Offaly, is thought to have been imported from eastern Gaul or the Middle Rhine. From about 900 BC, there was a fashion for solid bracelets and delicate ear spools. Men carried swords with golden hilts; their chariots, too, were inlaid with gold. Some of the furniture at the royal palace of Tara in County Meath was said to be made of pure gold. Evidently, the allure of gold also appealed to the next people to reach Ireland, the Celts.

5 The Bog Toghers

When our cars bounce along the bog roads of Ireland today we are often following the course of ancient highways that were laid down thousands of years ago. Known as 'toghers' (from the Gaelic word for 'causeway'), they range in date from the Neolithic and Bronze Age to the medieval period. Their purpose was to carry people safely across potentially treacherous bogs or to simply provide access to those peaty lands.

One such togher was recently found in the great Midlands bog at Mayne in County Westmeath. It follows a course of nearly 700 m (2,300 ft) through the bog to the River Inny, where what appears to be a platform of crossing timbers has also been identified. In the townland of Corralanna, just across the Inny, another oak-wood trackway runs directly in line with the Mayne togher, while a second road made of rougher brushwood runs parallel to it.

The Mayne togher consists of several thousand slender, hand-hewn oak planks that had been covered up by turf long centuries earlier. Each perfectly preserved plank measured between 4.3 m (14 ft) and 6 m (20 ft) in width; they had all been carefully shaped with slots for inserting holding posts. Axes and other stone tools found in the Corralanna bog are evidence of human activity in these parts from as far back as the late Mesolithic period, and yet it is perfectly possible that the Mayne togher was only in use for a handful of decades before it was subsumed into the bog; the surviving segments show no evidence of it ever having been repaired.

Preliminary carbon dating of the Mayne togher pegs it at 890 BC, which is about when the late Bronze Age starts turning into the early Iron Age. Early Irish folklore occasionally mentions such roads. In *Tochmarc Étaíne* (The Wooing of Étaín), Midir, a scion of the mythical Tuatha Dé Danann (People of the Goddess

Danu), oversees the construction of a bog road. 'You would have thought that every man in the world was there making noise,' the narrator remarks, as 'the trees of the forest, with their trunks and their roots' were converted into 'the foundation of the causeway', after which 'clay and gravel and stones were spread over the bog'. The tale also refers to oxen, yoked across the shoulders, who laid the trackway on top; one might have expected such robust beasts to sink into the bog.

The oak-wood planks used in the construction of the Mayne togher may have come from Lough Derravaragh, the 'lake of the oaks', which forms the southern border of the parish of Mayne. The lough is celebrated in Irish lore for its links to the mythical Children of Lir who spent three hundred years here in the guise of swans. Perhaps the Mayne togher is somehow connected to

the ancient passage tombs at Loughcrew, 25 km (15½ miles) east in County Meath where the Inny rises, or with a vanished road network connecting the revered hills of Tara, Ward, Skryne and Uisneach, all of which are found within this region. One thinks of the road upon which Túathal Techtmar, the vengeful son of a deposed High King of Ireland, marched his army to the Hill of Skryne to slay his enemies and reclaim the throne.

More than a hundred toghers have been identified in the Corlea bog in neighbouring County Longford, with the two oldest dated to about 3360 BC and 2260 BC respectively. Its most famous togher is the Corlea Trackway, known locally as the Danes' Road, which was constructed in a single year, c. 148–147 BC. Archaeologists estimate that three hundred oaks were felled to make the 1-km (⅔-mile) track, along with a similar number of birch trees for the rails on which the oak-wood planks were lain. Fragments of broken wheels found amid the planks trigger images of the mythological hero Cú Chulainn and other Celtic warriors racing chariots, perhaps seeking to compete in the Áenach Tailteann games at Teltown, County Meath.

We know almost nothing about the people who lived here at the time when the Mayne trackway was built but human sacrifice was certainly on the agenda. The Clonycavan Man, arguably the best preserved of Ireland's macabre 'bog bodies', was found at Ballivor, County Meath, 40 km (25 miles) southeast of Mayne. He had been whacked on the head with an axe three times, and then slashed across his chest before he was disembowelled. Rather fabulously, his spiky hairdo was attributed to a high-quality gel made of vegetable oil and pine resin that appears to have been imported from either southwest France or the north of Spain.

Or consider the Croghan Man whose brutally decapitated remains were found at Croghan Hill near Daingean, County

Offaly. Standing 1.98 m (6 ft 6 in) in his prime, he is thought to have been a citizen of high rank. His finely manicured finger-nails do not indicate a life of toil and his last meal was wheat and buttermilk, the Iron Age's answer to Weetabix. One theory holds that these ill-fated chaps were royals who were sacrificed by angry Druids in the wake of a bad harvest. Beholding them today in Dublin's National Museum of Ireland, it is extraordinary to imagine how these withered corpses journeyed upon roads just like the Mayne togher and the Corlea Trackway over two thousand years ago.

6 Roman Hibernia

 In AD 60, less than two decades after the Roman conquest of Celtic Britain, the governor of the new province, Gaius Suetonius Paulinus, marched on the sacred Welsh island of Mona, now known as Anglesey, with an army of perhaps twenty thousand legionaries. On behalf of his emperor, Nero, he sought to exterminate this 'refuge for fugitives', which also happened to be the greatest stronghold of Druidism in Britain. As the flat-bottomed boats carrying Paulinus's army arrived along Anglesey's shore, they were met by a mass of Druids, arms outstretched, roaring such 'dreadful imprecations' into the heavens above that the Romans were 'paralysed' with fear. It was only a momentary freeze. On Paulinus's command, the legionnaires surged forward and annihilated the Druids. As he watched his men destroy the holy groves over the ensuing days, Paulinus must have mused upon his prospects of extending the Roman Empire west across the tempestuous Irish Sea.

Less than 113 km (70 miles) from Anglesey was an island that the Roman historian Tacitus called Hibernia – the Land of Winter. The inhabitants of this land did not impress Pomponius Mela, a contemporary of Paulinus, who hailed from the Roman province of Baetica (now Andalusia) in southern Spain. He described them as 'a people wanting in every virtue, and totally destitute of piety', and yet this country was so 'luxuriant in grasses' that if cattle were 'allowed to feed too long, they would burst'. As it happened, all such temptations to advance on Ireland's green shores were hurled aside when Paulinus learned that Boudicca, queen of the Iceni, had seized the opportunity of his Welsh expedition to launch a major rebellion in southeast England. The governor glumly about-turned his army and headed onwards to resolve the situation.

The Romans never conquered Ireland. They did not even try. The closest they came was twenty years after the invasion of Anglesey when Agricola, another governor, eyeballed the north coast of Ulster from the 'trackless wastes' of Galloway in Scotland. According to Tacitus, Agricola's son-in-law, the governor brazenly remarked that Ireland could have been conquered and occupied by a single legion with a few auxiliaries. An exiled Irish prince was among Agricola's entourage, giving rise to the possibility that this was Túathal Techtmar, the son of a deposed High King of Ireland, who is said to have invaded Ireland from afar in order to regain his kingdom at about this time.

Some archaeologists have suggested that Agricola established a bridgehead at Drumanagh, an Iron Age promontory fort that juts into the Irish Sea near Rush, some 20 km (12½ miles) north of Dublin. The notion that Drumanagh was, at the very least, some form of Roman trading depot was boosted by the discovery of Roman coins, metalwork and tableware at the fort, including fragments of amphorae pottery from Pomponius Mela's homeland in Baetica. Whether Agricola went on the offensive or not, he certainly fortified parts of Britain's western shore against attacks from Ireland. Among the many reveals of the 2018 heatwave were the remains of a watchtower on the Llŷn Peninsula, just south of Anglesey, complete with barracks for a coastal garrison.

In AD 150, some sixty years after Agricola's death, the Greco-Egyptian writer Claudius Ptolemy devised what is ostensibly the first-known map of Ireland, shown in *Geographia*, an atlas of the Roman Empire and beyond. Ptolemy pinpointed a number of coastal settlements in Ireland, as well as royal settlements such as Emain Macha (Navan) in County Armagh. He also named sixteen Irish tribes, including the Voluntii of Ulster and the Gangani of Munster, who may have been connected to what Ptolemy calls the 'promontory of the Gangani' on Anglesey.

Ptolemy also located a tribe of Brigantes around present-day Wexford, Waterford and Kilkenny in southeast Ireland who were assumed to be close kin of the people of Brigantia in Britain, a territory centred on what is now Yorkshire that extended all the way to the west coast of Britain. Eight bodies buried on Lambay Island, located a short distance out to sea from the Drumanagh fort, are thought to have been British Brigantes on the run in about AD 74. It is quite plausible, in such seafaring times, that the same tribe dominated on both sides of the Irish Sea and, by extension, the central waterway itself.

Rome's failure to control the Irish Sea was to be the bane of many a governor of Roman Britain, as it provided a safe haven for incessant marauding pirates and other enemies of state. Tacitus was all in favour of the conquest of Ireland, arguing that it would increase the prosperity and security of the empire. 'We know

most of [Ireland's] harbours and approaches,' he wrote, 'and that through the intercourse of commerce.'

Roman Britain certainly traded with Ireland, exchanging metals, cattle, grain, animal hides, hunting dogs and human slaves for wine, olive oil and decorated craftware such as crockery, glasses, jewelry and ivory. Roman coins and jewelry have been found in prominent ancient strongholds such as Tara in County Meath and Cashel in County Tipperary, as well as in the passage tomb at Newgrange. Coins adorned with the heads of emperors Magnentius (AD 350–353) and Constantine the Great (AD 306–337) were also recovered from Ireland's Eye off the coast of County Dublin, and Dunsink and Malahide, on the nearby mainland.

The presence of Roman traders in Cork Harbour is suggested by a hoard of 3rd- and 4th-century Roman coins found at Cuskinny Marsh. Hoards of Roman silver and ingots have likewise been found at Balline, County Limerick, and Ballinrees, County Derry. There is also a certain amount of chin-stroking over a Roman-style cremation that took place at Stoneyford, County Kilkenny, in the 1st century AD. Roman coins found in a grave at Bray Head, County Wicklow, are assumed to have been a down-payment for the ferryman to transport the deceased safely to the afterlife, while a single Roman coin found at Mullaghmast in County Kildare may have been a memento from a pilgrimage that served as a talisman on a long-gone abode.

In AD 391, Quintus Aurelius Symmachus, a Roman consul, dispatched a thank-you letter to his friend, Flavianus: 'In order to win the favour of the Roman people for our Quaestor, you have been a generous and diligent provider of novel contributions to our solemn shows and games, as is proved by your gift of seven Irish dogs. All Rome viewed them with wonder, and fancied they must have been brought hither in iron cages. For such a gift I tender you the greatest possible thanks.' It is assumed that these 'Irish dogs' were Irish wolfhounds whose luckless destiny was to take their chances against bears, lions and gladiators in the arenas of Rome.

One of Ireland's larger commodities at this time was human slaves. The country was a prominent slave-trading centre and many of the slaves who worked on the farms of the wealthy villa-owning elite in Roman Britain are thought to have started life in Hibernia. With the sharp decline of the Roman Empire during the 5th century, the tables were turned, with captives from Britain now heading west across the Irish Sea to work as slaves on Irish farms. By far the most famous of these was St Patrick, the son of a Roman decurion, or tax collector, who was apparently swiped by pirates from an as yet unidentified part of Britain's shoreline in about AD 415. Ireland's position as a major maritime slave-trading hub was later reignited during the Viking Age.

In time, St Patrick would be credited with persuading the monarchs of Ireland to cast aside their Druids in favour of a carpenter's son from Galilee who had been put to death by the Romans. There were, in fact, Christians in Ireland before Patrick's time, particularly in County Wexford. In 431, a year before Patrick's Irish mission began, Palladius, the son of a Gaulish noble from Poitiers in France, was apparently sent by the Pope to administer to Ireland's small Christian community. Although he is acknowledged as the 'first Bishop to the Irish believing in Christ', Palladius quit within a year, miffed that the indigenous people were so immune to his charms.

Perhaps St Patrick's greatest challenge was to bring an end to the age of Druids, who had been in the ascendance since the late Iron Age; their deepest roots stretched back to the erudite architects of the Neolithic passage tombs. As well versed in natural philosophy as they were in politics, the law and education, these remarkable people were also doyens of astronomy, herb lore and oral tradition. Druids are credited with creating the ogham alphabet, having apparently been inspired by the Latin alphabet introduced to Britain by the Romans. For their part, the Romans would claim that the Druids were demonic brutes who strangled, drowned and otherwise murdered innocent people to appease their gods; the bodies of sacrificial victims found in the Irish bogs suggest that this Roman view was not entirely far-fetched.

The Druidic culture remained in Irish consciousness long after Druids themselves had been eradicated as a major force. Indeed, Ireland's Bardic tradition can very much be construed as an element of the oral culture of Druidism, while the yew trees that adorn church cemeteries to this day were likewise venerated by the Druids. The crossover between the two cultures is exemplified by the tale of St Brigid of Kildare, another of Ireland's patron saints, who was raised in a Druidic household in the 7th century.

Christianity – and the Roman Catholic Church that it spawned – was by far the most enduring legacy of the Roman age in Ireland. The Catholic Church itself is heavily based on the hierarchical, centralized Roman system, despite the fact that the Western Roman Empire had collapsed by the time it came into being. After its downfall in the mid 5th century, the centre of cultural gravity moved eastwards to Byzantium (Constantinople, now Istanbul). Celtic interlace manuscripts like the Book of Durrow and the Book of Kells may have drawn inspiration from the artistic tradition of the Eastern Roman Empire in Byzantium and Syria, where illuminated texts were produced during the 5th and 6th centuries.

At the same time, much of the knowledge and learning gathered during the Roman age would, in turn, be preserved in monasteries across Ireland during the 5th, 6th and 7th centuries.

7 Pagan Christians & Holy Wells

Humans have always sought the curative qualities of water. The Celtic legends extol sacred rivers like the Boyne and the Shannon for bestowing life, wisdom and beauty on the warriors and queens of old. Wells and other springs of pure water were likewise deemed to bubble up from the Otherworld. They were often dedicated to pagan deities like Bríd, the Celtic goddess of inspiration, healing and smith-craft, or Danu, goddess of the Tuatha Dé Danann.

Wells were of paramount importance to the people of Ireland, who flocked to them for supernatural protection, respectful of the water's ability to alleviate toothache and gammy eyes. The sick and the wounded were brought to these hallowed springs where their afflicted bodies were rubbed with rag cloths soaked in the holy water. The rag was then tied to a nearby tree, the concept being that the malady would now politely exit the body and resettle in the cloth. This must have resulted in endless disappointment but, nonetheless, early Christians adopted the wells, which were, in time, rebranded as 'holy wells' or 'blessed wells'. Wherever there is a holy well in Ireland, you can be sure a monastery of some shape or other once stood in close proximity.

The Republic of Ireland's National Monuments Service has a record of approximately 3,000 holy wells, based on the Ordnance Survey's findings throughout the island between 1824 and 1846, but it is likely there were far more than that a thousand years ago. Although some are natural, the majority are man-made. They sprawl across hilltops and waysides, sink deep within forests and plains, and lie buried on hillsides and remote islands. At least 330 holy wells have been documented in County Clare, with 40 lying amid the cavernous limestone region of the Burren. Another 128 wells have so far been identified in County Dublin, of which about 100 survive in one form or another.

Under the Christians, most wells were rededicated to a particular Irish saint, such as St Brigid, who was assigned all of those wells where the goddess Bríd had been worshipped. Danu, whose day was celebrated in May, likewise metamorphosed into St Ann. Aside from St Brigid, St Ann and the Virgin Mary, the saints ascribed to holy wells were predominantly male, with St Patrick inevitably topping the charts by some distance.

When it came to a particular saint's feast day, the multitudes would assemble by the well for what became known as the 'pattern', from the Irish word *pátrún* ('patron saint'). Our word 'holiday' also comes direct from these 'holy days'. For some, the pattern involved circumambulating the well an odd number of times (usually three, seven, nine or fifteen) in a clockwise direction, while reciting devotional or penitential prayers and charms. These were the 'stations' (*turas*); people kept count by dropping pebbles on a pile each time they completed a round. To boost your chances of having your sins remitted, you could increase

your pain levels by doing it all barefoot or on your knees. It was also whispered that if you reversed the direction of the stations, you could inflict a curse on an enemy, but you were warned that the jinx could backfire if God deemed your curse unjustified.

Others came to be healed, just as their ancestors had done thousands of years before. In the 13th century, many holy wells were dedicated to St John, the patron saint of the Knights of St John of Jerusalem, whose hospitals and infirmaries were often established beside such springs. Some wells were considered especially good for specific ailments – rheumatism, worms, anxiety – while, in a further nod to pagan times, the supernatural rag tree also continued. Tellingly, many patterns took place in August, formerly the month of the pre-Christian festival of Lughnasa.

For many, the pattern meant party time. So much so that in 1660, a dour Synod of the Catholic Province of Tuam outlawed 'dancing, flute-playing, singing in harmony, intermingling and other such abuses…during the visitation of wells and other holy places'. In 1703 one of the anti-Catholic Penal Laws confronted 'the superstitions of popery' that, according to the Act, were 'greatly increased by the pretended sanctity…of wells to which pilgrimages are made by vast numbers'. Under the terms of the Act, 'all such meetings and assembles shall be adjudged riots, and unlawful assemblies, and punishable as such'. Those who breached the law were hit with a 10 shilling fine, increasing to 20 shillings if caught selling 'ale, victuals or other commodities'. Anyone who did not have the money to pay up could be subject to a public flogging.

None of this stopped ten thousand pilgrims turning up at St John's Well at Warrenstown, County Meath, on St John's Day, 24 June 1710. However, four years later, the High Sheriff of County Wicklow gleefully described the fate of a similar pilgrimage to Glendalough when his men 'destroyed the wells' and 'demolished their superstitious crosses'. Only two of the holy wells at Glendalough have survived to the present day.

In truth, most landowners turned a blind eye when people gathered at these spiritual wells. With Catholic churches effectively outlawed, holy wells remained *the* place to go for prayers, ritual observance and, indeed, dancing throughout the 18th century. In 1813, the antiquary Thomas Crofton Croker attended a Pattern Day in County Kerry where he observed: 'After having satisfied our mental craving, we felt it necessary to attend to our bodily appetites, and for this purpose adjourned to a tent where some tempting slices of curdy Kerry salmon had attracted our notice.... After discussing the merits of this salmon, and washing it down with some of "Beamish & Crawford's Porter" we whiled away the time by drinking whiskey-punch, observing the dancing to an excellent piper, and listening to the songs and story-telling which were going on about us.'

The Catholic Church, however, became increasingly hostile to holy wells during the 19th century. In part, the hierarchy was uneasy at the fragility of the Christian veneer covering the island's pagan roots, but they were also appalled by the boorishness and drunken brawling that were so often on display at patterns. Moreover, after Catholic emancipation in 1829, the increasingly educated Catholic populace were eager to worship in the handsome new Catholic churches rather than meet by the same old wells. The church wrestled control of the patterns, which were reformed as officially approved parochial festivals, including St Patrick's Day, Easter and Christmas.

Only a handful of local saints are still commemorated in 21st-century Ireland. The ever-dwindling crowd that visit

St John's Well at Warrenstown on 24 June will not have taken heart from the startling removal of its surrounding wall and steps in 2018. The cult of holy wells has also all but vanished although one still sees the occasional rag tree, its branches emblazoned with sweet wrappers and modern-day rags, or wells sprinkled with fresh (or plastic) flowers, pebbles and rosary beads.

8 High Crosses of the Kingdom of Ossory

 Cerball mac Dúnlainge was one of the most powerful kings in Ireland during the late 9th century but few have heard of the kingdom of Ossory over which he ruled for forty-six years. Ossory occupied most of present-day County Kilkenny, as well as large chunks of counties Laois and Offaly. It had been part of the kingdom of Munster until Cerball engineered a sort of Brexit manoeuvre and secured semi-independence. His descendants would later adopt the surname Mac Giolla Phádraig, although his kingdom went into swift decline after the Cambro-Norman invasion.

Cerball's frequent victories over his Viking enemies earned him several stanzas in the Icelandic Sagas, but his defining legacy is a remarkable collection of Christian crosses that were carved from stone at the height of his reign nearly twelve hundred years ago. The oldest of these iconic works are to be found at Ahenny near the Lingaun River in County Tipperary. Two high crosses, carved from sandstone, stand in a graveyard beside a ruined church; both are studded with five gems, recalling the five wounds that Jesus Christ received on the cross – the nails in his feet and hands, and the spear wound in his left side. There is a hint of the Pict about the art at the base of the Ahenny crosses as well as a continental influence in the overall ecclesiastical iconography; the decoration includes the earliest Irish image of a chariot.

Three more high crosses stand a few kilometres south at Kilkieran, County Kilkenny, named for St Kieran, the son of an Ossory nobleman, who returned from studies in Tours, France, and Rome to set up a monastery at Saighir in the Slieve Bloom Mountains. Cerball and many other kings of Ossory were buried at Saighir. Just before Kieran was conceived, his mother dreamt that a star fell into her mouth; the Druids told her she would bear a son whose renown and virtues would reach the world's end. Kieran certainly did what he could to fulfil his mother's dreams; his neatest trick was to bless a well so that its water tasted like both wine and honey at once, enabling partakers to become 'drunk as well as filled'.

Arguably the finest of the Ossory high crosses is found amid the tranquil, ivy-strewn ruins of Killamery, near the eastern bank of the Lingaun in County Kilkenny. Founded by St Gobban, the monastic school at Killamery was reputedly home to a thousand monks in the 7th century. The 9th-century mossy high cross is thought to offer 'A Prayer for Máel Sechnaill', Cerball's father-in-law, who was High King of Ireland from 846 to 862. It also boasts a motif that is perhaps the most instantly recognizable image of 'Irishness' in the world today: the sun cross, a mainstay of Celtic jewelry, as well as gravestones across the globe. The circle, connecting the four arms of the cross, represents eternal life and God's infinite love, as well as being a pagan nod to the sun itself. The Killamery cross is also known as the Snake-Dragon Cross

because of its pattern of interlacing snakes and, above the boss, an open-mouthed dragon.

Some believe these patterns were originally painted in bright colours – akin to the brilliant hues of the Book of Kells perhaps – so that each cross looked as if it was made of gold and covered in jewels. There is also a theory that many of these crosses were the work of a single, prolific but anonymous master sculptor. In any event, these incredible crosses represent an age when Ireland – and Ossory in particular – shone a powerful light for the future of both Christianity and decorative art.

9 The Uí Dúnlainge Kings of Leinster

Fergal mac Máele Dúin was into his twelfth year as High King of Ireland when he marched a massive force of the Uí Néill south to confront the Laigin (Leinstermen) by the Hill of Allen in County Kildare. Details elude us but the battle that these two mighty armies fought on 11 December 722 was an unmitigated disaster for the invaders – Fergal was slain alongside many Uí Néill nobles.

Murchad mac Brain Mut, the victorious king of Leinster, hailed from the Uí Dúnlainge dynasty. Their rise to power was further boosted by the annihilation of their arch-rivals, the Uí Cheinnselaig, at the Battle of the Groans near Carbury, County Kildare, in 738. According to the Annals of Ulster, 'so many fell in this great battle that we find no comparable slaughter in a single onslaught'. The Uí Dúnlainge were to maintain a vice-like grip over the kingship of Leinster for the next three centuries, although there was much in-fighting as the throne rotated between three septs, or clans, within the dynasty.

The most northerly of the three septs were the Uí Dúnchada, who had their inauguration site at Lyons Hill on the Dublin–Kildare border. They also held the abbacy of Kildare, a lucrative office given that this was the age in which the number of pilgrims venerating the cult of St Brigid was at its peak. The Uí Dúnchada provided ten kings of Leinster; the last had the thankless task of trying, in vain, to halt the unstoppable tide of Brian Boru's Munster army as it marched through his kingdom to seize control of Viking Dublin (see chapter 10).

The Uí Fáeláin kings of Leinster, ancestors of the O'Byrnes, ruled from their stronghold at Naas (Nás na Ríogh, 'the place of kings') in present-day County Kildare, and provided nine monarchs for Leinster. One of the last Uí Fáeláin kings was Cerball mac Muirecáin, 'a skilful horseman', who expelled the Norse from Dublin City in 902. Six years later, he led his army out to join those of Flann Sinna, the High King of Ireland, and Cathal mac Conchobair, the king of Connacht. Opposing them was the army of Cerball's foster-brother, Cormac mac Cuilennáin, king of Munster, who was hailed by his contemporaries as 'a scholar in Irish and in Latin, the wholly pious and pure chief bishop, miraculous in chastity and in prayer'. His works are said to have included the *Sanas Cormaic* (Cormac's Glossary) and the now-lost *Psalter of Cashel*. Cormac did not wish to fight but he had been cajoled into war by his sinister advisor, Flaithbertach. Cormac's hesitancy was shared by his men, not least when Flaithbertach had an embarrassing tumble from his horse at the muster before the battle.

On 13 September 908, the two armies met at Bellaghmoon, near Castledermot in County Kildare, where Cormac had apparently been educated by Snerdgus, the abbot of Díseart Díarmada (Castledermot), in calmer times. The ill omen that befell Flaithbertach prior to the battle proved the foretaste of a decisive

victory for Cerball and Flann Sinna. The saintly Cormac was among those killed, his neck broken when he, too, fell from his horse. His severed head was triumphantly presented to Flann but the elderly High King was unimpressed. He is said to have denounced the beheading of the 'holy bishop' as an evil deed, before gripping it in his hands and showering it with kisses.

After his victory at Bellaghmoon, Cerball was escorting a group of high-ranking prisoners through the ecclesiastical city of Kildare when a spark from a blacksmith's forge caused his horse to shy; the Leinster king was flung upon his own lance and subsequently died in Naas from his wounds. He was buried at Cill Corban near Kill, as were eight previous kings before him.

The Uí Muiredaig sept, who provided fourteen kings, were headquartered in the hillfort at Mullaghmast in the south of County Kildare. The Mullaghmast Stone, a limestone boulder decorated with pre-Christian spirals by a 6th-century-AD carver, served as their coronation stone and is now held at the National Museum in Dublin. Some of the kings may have been inaugurated on the summit of the nearby rath (ringfort) at Mullaghreelan. This branch of the Uí Dúnlainge later adopted the name O'Toole (Ua Tuathail), after Tuathal mac Augaire, king of Leinster, who died in 958. St Laurence O'Toole, archbishop of Dublin, was reputedly born at Mullaghreelan in 1128, as was his half-sister Mór, the wife of Dermot MacMurrough, king of Leinster. Dermot and Mór's daughter Aoife married Richard de Clare, Earl of Pembroke, a Cambro-Norman warrior known to posterity as Strongbow (see chapter 11). The O'Tooles were to be displaced from Mullaghmast by Sir Walter de Riddlesford, one of Strongbow's chainmail-clad allies, after which they established a new power base in the Glen of Imaal in the Wicklow Mountains.

10 Sitric Silkbeard & Queen Gormflaith

It's not every day that your mother marries your arch-nemesis and that you then marry his daughter. But that's precisely what happened to Sitric Silkbeard, king of Dublin, who thus became both stepson and son-in-law to no less a warrior than Brian Boru, the most famous High King in Irish history.

Sitric Silkbeard reigned over the Viking city of Dublin for almost half a century. As well as being a survivor of the Battle of Clontarf, he founded Christ Church Cathedral and Ireland's first ever mint. At the time of his birth in about 970, Dublin was one of Europe's preeminent trading cities, not least as a holding depot for slaves. Coastal communities lay in icy fear of Viking slavers, such as the fleet of two hundred longships that once sailed into Dublin Bay from Alba (Scotland) 'bringing away with them in captivity to Ireland a great prey of Angles and Britons and Picts'. Sitric was named for his grandfather Sitriuc, a scion of the formidable royal Norse dynasty of Uí Ímair, which controlled much of the Irish Sea in the 10th century, including the west coast of Scotland, the Hebrides and parts of northern England.

In 917, the elder Sitriuc added the kingdom of Dublin to his possessions. His son Amlaíb (also known as Olaf Cuarán) duly became king of Dublin and married Gormflaith, daughter of the king of Leinster. Sitric was their only son. Amlaíb's reign ended dismally when his son-in-law Máel Sechnaill, the High King of Ireland, destroyed the Dubliners in a battle at the Hill of Tara in 980. The High King's conquering forces then occupied Dublin, where Máel Sechnaill proclaimed the city's slaves to be free and exacted a hefty tax upon its citizens. In defeat, Amlaíb abdicated in favour of his son Glúniairn ('Iron-knee') and retreated to the monastery on the Scottish island of Iona that had been founded by St Columba more than four hundred years earlier. He died soon after his arrival.

As a boy, Sitric Silkbeard had watched his father's reign collapse in disarray. Things did not improve under his drink-addled

half-brother Glúniairn whose nine-year rule concluded when he was murdered in a haze of intoxication by a slave called Colban. It is thought that Dublin then became the stronghold of the powerful Olaf Tryggvason, a future king of Norway, who spent five years wearing down various opponents around Leinster. After Olaf's return to Norway, Dublin was briefly ruled by Ivar, the Norse king of Waterford, but by 993 Sitric had claimed the kingship of Dublin for himself. More warfare with neighbouring kings ensued; churches burned, warriors died, hostages, horses and cattle were exchanged. On one occasion, Máel Sechnaill returned to Dublin and seized the sacred Ring of Tomar and the Sword of Carlus, two highly prized Viking heirlooms.

Sitric was not an idle monarch. In about 995 he founded a mint in Dublin. Deducing that such coinage would inspire further raids on his vulnerable kingdom, he either constructed or augmented a series of timber walls and earthen embankments around Dublin that formed the basis for the city's first stone wall a

century later. He also formed a strategic alliance with his uncle, Máel Mórda, king of Leinster, in the hope that their combined forces might halt the rapidly advancing army of Brian Boru, king of Munster.

It was not to be. In 999, the Munster men tore through the armies of both Sitric and Máel Mórda at the Battle of Glenmama near Lyons Hill, County Kildare, after which they stormed Dublin, burned down the city and expelled Sitric. As part of the peace process that followed Sitric's submission, Brian Boru married Sitric's widowed mother Gormflaith while Sitric was himself wed to Brian's daughter Sláine.

Three years later, Brian Boru marched north, overthrew Máel Sechnaill and claimed the high kingship. At this time, Sitric joined the Munster army and, following a series of campaigns into Ulster, the northern Uí Néill were cajoled into acknowledging Brian as High King. A period of relative peace and prosperity followed. Archaeological digs have unearthed enough ships, gold, coins and clothing to justify the depiction of Dublin by contemporary sagas as a frenetic and booming port.

The good times did not last long. Even as the Uí Néill were hailing Brian Boru as High King, things were on the slide. Medieval posterity would inevitably blame it on a woman, namely Gormflaith, mother of Sitric, who was all too soon to become Brian Boru's *ex*-wife. She is consistently lambasted as a villain in medieval folklore. For instance, the 13th-century Icelandic *Njál's Saga* describes her as 'a very beautiful woman...and it was commonly said that her character was evil insofar as she had control over it'. In fairness to Gormflaith, no record of her appeared on paper until six decades after her death. Her resurrection as the wicked femme fatale can be traced to *Cogad Gáedel re Gallaib* (The War of the Irish with the Foreigners), a propaganda-heavy account commissioned by one of Brian Boru's descendants almost a hundred years after the events took place. Nonetheless, the story runs that after Gormflaith and Brian Boru's messy divorce, Gormflaith goaded her son Sitric and her brother Máel Mórda into their doomed war with her former husband.

Things began to go downhill for the Leinster–Viking alliance in 1013 when Sitric's son Oleif was killed in the aftermath of an unsuccessful attack on Brian Boru's fleet at Cape Clear in West Cork, On Good Friday 1014, the opposing armies met at Clontarf, near Dublin. Sitric appears to have sagely stood well back from the action while thousands of men chopped and stabbed one another to death. It was to be a convincing victory for the Munster men and their allies, although the dead would include both Máel Mórda and Brian Boru.

As the dust settled, Sitric returned to his Dublin kingdom, but hopes for a trouble-free future were dashed by the combination of a plague epidemic and the resurgence of Máel Sechnaill, the ousted High King, who burned the suburbs of Dublin to a crisp. Whenever the contest for the high kingship heated up, the wealthy port of Dublin became the must-have jewel in any aspiring king's crown. As such, the city was constantly raided and its citizens taken hostage. In response, Sitric turned tonto, blinding his own hostages and marching out to plunder his enemies. He wasn't very good at it; the new king of Leinster pulverized his army at Delgany in County Wicklow and his fleet was decimated by the men of Ulster off the coast of County Down.

In 1028, Sitric went on a pilgrimage to Rome but his prayers failed to prevent his son Amlaíb from being captured; Sitric was forced to hand over 1,200 cows, 140 Welsh horses, 1.87 kg (60 oz t) of gold, 1.87 kg (60 oz t) of silver and the Sword of Carlus, as well as returning most of the hostages he held.

The 1030s were better years, largely because he teamed up with Cnut the Great, aka Canute, the king of Denmark, England, Norway and parts of Sweden. Their combined fleets raided Wales and Sitric established a Viking colony near Llandwrog in Gwynedd. In 2015, this colony re-emerged from obscurity when a treasure hunter found a hoard of fourteen silver pennies that had been minted in Dublin during Sitric's reign; eight dated from the late 990s while the other six were from about 1018.

Some of the coins Sitric minted bore the sign of the cross. It was during the latter part of his reign that he made Dublin into a bishopric, based on the Roman model, and commissioned the first timber and stone structure of Christ Church Cathedral (it was rebuilt by the Anglo-Normans in the 1180s). Such developments proved a massive step in converting Dublin from a pagan city into a Christian one.

Not that Sitric was ever much of a loving Christian to his neighbours. After one towering victory in 1032, he burned alive two hundred of his enemies in the stone church at Ardbraccan, County Meath, and took another two hundred as slaves. He pushed it too far when he executed Ragnall, king of Waterford, on his return from Ardbraccan. The death of Canute soon afterwards deprived him of his only influential ally. Echmarcach, king of the Isles, promptly invaded Dublin and forced Sitric to abdicate; Echmarcach may well have been King Ragnall's son.

Sitric lived until 1042; his place of death is unknown. His son Amlaíb (also known as Olaf Sigtryggsson) was slain by Saxons while on a pilgrimage to Rome in 1034 but Sitric's blood would live on through Amlaíb's sole surviving child, a daughter named Ragnailt. Her Dublin-born son Gruffudd ap Cynan became king of Gwynedd and was great-grandfather to Llywelyn the Great, one of the most formidable rulers in Welsh history.

11 The Knights Templar of Ireland

The Knights Templar have captivated people's imagination ever since the uber-wealthy military order was founded in 1119. Their initial purpose was to prevent pilgrims from being mugged and murdered by brigands on the roads leading into the Holy City of Jerusalem, which was then under Norman control. The order came to prominence during the Second Crusade when Templars saved the French king's life. By the time of the Cambro-Norman invasion of Ireland in 1169, the Templars formed the elite of the crusading armies.

The order also bankrolled the Crusades, serving as both bankers and counsellors to many European monarchs. It offered a wide range of financial services including large-scale estate management, raising of loans, tax collection, rock-solid security vaults and the safe transportation of vast sums of money, courtesy of an exceptionally adept fleet. Eight hundred years ago, it was possible to deposit money in one Templar preceptory in return for a letter of receipt that could be used to withdraw money from another. At its peak, the order had over four thousand people working at its financial headquarters in Paris. Not surprisingly, the master of the Knights Templar in Ireland was also an auditor of the Irish Exchequer.

Among the most potent Knights Templar in England was Geoffrey Fitz Stephen, its master from 1180 to 1185. He may well have been a brother or close kinsman of the adventurer Robert FitzStephen, who landed at Bannow Island in County Wexford in early May 1169 with a mercenary force of thirty knights, sixty men-at-arms and three hundred archers. The following day a further ten knights, thirty men-at-arms and one hundred archers arrived with FitzStephen's half-brother Maurice FitzGerald, the founding father of the celebrated Irish dynasty of FitzGerald. Their arrival, just over 850 years ago, marked the start of the Cambro-Norman advance on Ireland.

The first documented evidence of Templars in Ireland is from 1177, less than a decade after the Normans arrived, when 'Matthew the Templar' witnessed a charter connected to Christ Church Cathedral, Dublin. In about 1183, Walter de Riddlesford, Lord of Bray, became the first of thirteen Masters of the Knights Templar in Ireland. Riddlesford, who was also part of the initial Norman invasion force, is said to have founded a Templar base at Castledermot in County Kildare. He lived at Kilkea Castle, near Castledermot, which was built for him by Hugh de Lacy, described by his contemporary Giraldus Cambrensis as 'a swarthy man with small, black deep-set eyes, a flat nose, an ugly scar on his right cheek caused by a burn, a short neck and a hairy sinewy body'.

De Lacy may not have been a pretty sight but he was a formidable castle builder; his other legacies include Trim Castle

in County Meath (which doubled up as York in Mel Gibson's Oscar-winning epic *Braveheart*) and Clontarf Castle (which became the headquarters of the Knights Templar in Ireland). Hugh's father Gilbert de Lacy, the 'crafty and sharp' precentor of the Knights Templar in Tripoli (Libya), was one of the most effective early Templars. In 1163, Gilbert commanded part of the Crusader army when it won a rare victory over Nur ad-Din, ruler of the Syrian province of the Seljuk Empire.

In about 1180, Henry II gave the Templars the 'vills' (taxable settlements) of both Clontarf and Crook, County Waterford, along with about 485 hectares (1,200 acres). The Templars owned at least eleven more preceptories and manors, primarily in counties Wexford, Waterford, Carlow, Dublin, Louth, Tipperary and Kilkenny. Its most westerly stronghold was by present-day Temple House in County Sligo, constructed under the patronage of the Bourke family. In 1301, Matilda de Lacy, the family matriarch, gifted the order the Templetown estate on the Cooley Peninsula in County Louth, which is said to have been the Templars' wealthiest manor.

The Templar's role in Ireland was primarily to raise income from agriculture and rents on its extensive estates in order to help fund campaigns in the Holy Land. To this end, it converted pasture into profitable cornfields, developed a modest cloth and wool industry and quite possibly bred horses. The men who ran these estates and collected the rents may well have been 'retired' Templars whose fighting days were behind them.

In 1219 the Templars achieved a major publicity coup when William Marshal, the richest knight in Britain or Ireland, was buried in the Temple Church in London, where his tomb can still be seen today. Like Henry II, Marshal appointed a Templar as his almoner, the man responsible for ensuring charity was distributed to the poor on his behalf. Marshal's wife Isabel was the daughter and sole heiress of that famous marriage between Richard de Clare (later known as Strongbow) and Aoife, the daughter of Dermot MacMurrough, king of Leinster. Having inherited what now became the lordship of Leinster, Marshal rebuilt the castles at Kilkenny, Carlow (see page 79) and, in County Wexford, Ferns and Enniscorthy, as well as the port at Clonmines and the Tower of Hook, said to be the world's oldest operational lighthouse. The Marshals also founded the Cistercian abbeys at Tintern, County Wexford, and Duiske, County Kilkenny, while their greatest legacy was the port town of New Ross in County Wexford, laid out on a grid, complete with bridge, walls, church and castle, to make what one contemporary described as 'a lovely city on the banks of the Barrow'.

The Templars continued to be a powerhouse for the remainder of the 13th century, serving as advisors to popes and kings, but their immense wealth diluted the order's once fanatical devotion to obedience, poverty and chastity. Moreover, the waning influence of the Christian kingdoms in the Middle East reached a new nadir in 1291 when the Mamluk Sultanate of Egypt under Saladin captured the city of Acre, thus removing the last traces of a Crusader state. Once Europe's most powerful military order, the Templars were now devoid of a purpose.

The Templars foremost enemy was Philip the Fair, the ironically named king of France, who had borrowed a good deal of money from them. Having already expelled one hundred thousand Jews from France, he now turned on his bankers. The purge began on Friday, 13 October 1307 with the mass arrest of Templars across France. Less than four months later, Edward II, King of England and Lord of Ireland, followed suit. John de Wogan, justiciar of Ireland, was instructed to place fourteen of Ireland's twenty or so Templar knights in custody in Dublin Castle and to make an inventory of their Irish possessions. The knights were hauled into St Patrick's Cathedral to answer eighty-five charges, including denying Christ, spitting on the cross, worshipping false idols and homosexuality.

The four-month inquisition of the Irish Templars was presided over by a troika of papal delegates from England who heard the testimonies of forty-one witnesses, including three prominent Dominican friars, two Franciscans and two Augustinians. Neither the Dominicans nor the Franciscans owed the Templars any favours; the Knights Templar was perceived as an English order and Irish friars had plenty of cause to be chary of its members' wealth and privileges. There was also still the shadow of Walter le Bachelor, master of the Irish Templars from 1295 to 1301, who had been found guilty of financial malpractice and died under suspicious circumstances in a Templar penitentiary in London.

The most controversial aspect of the trial concerned Henry Danet, who had taken office as master of the Templars in Ireland just two days before the arrests began. Danet, a veteran of both Cyprus and Syria, had been a favourite of Jacques de Molay, the order's disgraced Grand Master. Subjected to vicious torture, de Molay had already confessed to various heresies. Two witnesses suggested that Danet and de Molay had engaged in sodomy. Danet's cryptic defence was to damn the order's practices in faraway lands while insisting there was no untoward behaviour in Ireland. One can but imagine the tittle-tattle whistling through the streets of Dublin as these monks assembled day after day for the trial in the cathedral, which then lay just outside the city walls.

Meanwhile, life for the Templars went from bad to worse when Pope Clement V, a puppet of the French king, dissolved the entire order in 1311. Tortured for their 'abominations', the Templars were now thoroughly shamed and discredited. Jacques de Molay was among nearly a hundred Templars burned at the stake.

The Irish Templars strongly denied all charges. Unlike their French brethren, they were not tortured in order to extricate a confession. Moreover, it transpired that few witnesses were able to provide any real evidence of heretical wrongdoing. The most damning statement that could be mustered was from Friar Hugo de Lummour, who claimed he had once been at the Templar preceptory in Clontarf when he witnessed William de Warecome, a Templar knight, 'bend his head at the elevation of the sacrament, not caring to look at the host'. Nobody could construe this as evidence that the spirit of Beelzebub had taken root and, as such, the Irish Templars fared considerably better than their European counterparts.

When the trial concluded, the sturdiest penalty imposed was that the accused should do penance and, once absolved, they were pensioned off and appear to have retreated into monastic retirement ever after. Danet was released on bail. The Templars' estates were nonetheless seized and ultimately handed over to their arch-rivals, the Knights Hospitaller.

One notable legacy of the Templar trials concerns a Franciscan friar by the name of Richard Ledrede who was at the papal court in France when the Templars were being suppressed. In 1317 he was made bishop of Ossory in Ireland. Seven years later, he oversaw the trial in Kilkenny of Dame Alice Kyteler and various others for witchcraft; the suspects were subjected to similar torture to that which the Templars had suffered in France. One poor woman, Petronella di Midia, was burned at the stake with Ledrede watching her through the roaring flames.

12 Rohesia's Castle

 Castle Roche stands about 11 km (7 miles) northwest of Dundalk in County Louth, in what some might consider to be the middle of nowhere. However, this fortress was once of pivotal importance to the powers that were. It presided over the northern frontier between the Anglo-Norman-controlled Pale and the crumbling Gaelic kingdom of Ulaid in present-day Northern Ireland. It should really be called Rohesia's Castle after Rohesia de Verdon, the feisty lady who orchestrated its construction when she inherited these lands during the early 13th century.

Born in about 1200, Rohesia was a well-connected lady. Bertram de Verdon, her Anglo-Norman grandfather, had arrived in Ireland alongside the future King John in 1185 and acquired a good deal of land. Considered a good catch, Rohesia was obliged to ditch her first husband John de Bellew 'at the special request of the King' (aka Henry III), who decreed that she be wedded instead to Theobald Butler, the monarch's Chief Butler

in Ireland. She bore Theobald two sons and two daughters before he died in Poitou, France, in 1230 while serving with his monarch in the Gascon Campaign. Theobald's remains were returned for burial at the abbey in Arklow, County Wicklow, where he would later be joined by his son and grandson, the 3rd and 4th Chief Butlers respectively.

Meanwhile, his ambitious widow decided to build herself a castle. The story runs that nobody was willing to work for Rohesia because of her lousy temper. At length she made an offer to marry whosoever built her a castle. Given that she was a wealthy heiress, this was no mean proposition. The winner was the unnamed architect of Castle Roche, an impregnable bastion situated high upon a limestone outcrop. Shortly after Rohesia and her new husband moved in, she is said to have invited him to behold the majestic view from the highest window in the castle's banquet hall, where she shoved him out and watched him fall to his doom.

It's a good story but it transpires that Rohesia only married twice and both her husbands were dead when the castle was completed in 1236. The banquet hall where the so-called 'Murder Window' is located was not built until her son John de Verdon reached his majority in around 1240. Rohesia later became a nun at the Grace Dieu Priory in Leicestershire, England, where she died in 1247. She was buried in nearby Belton where her effigy can be seen in the parish church to this day.

Castle Roche, which appears to be based upon the English castle of Beeston in Cheshire, served as a vital strategic stronghold on the frontier between Ulster and the Pale, controlling the pass into what is now South Armagh. The de Verdon family remained there for several generations but the castle itself had been abandoned by the time the forces of that arch-castle-thrasher Oliver Cromwell directed a few token cannon balls at it in the 1640s. What remains today is as good a castellated ruin as you will find in Ireland.

13 Great Scot: Edward the Bruce's Invasion of Ireland

Edward II did not have much cause to celebrate during his reign as king of England. However, his mood must have been singularly improved by the arrival of a package from Ireland in October 1318. It contained the head of Edward the Bruce, a Scottish warlord who had caused the English monarch considerable indigestion by crowning himself High King of Ireland two years earlier.

Not that the famously feeble Edward II expected anything but hardship from the family of Robert the Bruce, king of Scots, who gave the English such a drubbing at the Battle of Bannockburn in 1314. In the wake of Bannockburn, King Robert dispatched his younger brother Edward to Ireland with a force of six thousand men. Their goal was to forge a Scots–Irish alliance that would oust the Anglo-Norman barons and establish a 'Pan-Gaelic Greater Scotia', in which the Bruce family would rule over Scotland, Ireland and, in due course, Wales.

Even as the Scottish army disembarked along the Antrim coast, the Bruces' propaganda gurus were highlighting the family's Irish lineage, harking back to a rather tentative claim to the dormant high kingship through Edward's grandmother, a descendant of Dermot MacMurrough, king of Leinster. Edward also carried a letter from King Robert, addressed to the leading Irish kings and chieftains, which spoke of the Scots and the Irish as '*nostra nacio* [our nation]...stemming from one seed of birth', united 'by a common language and by common custom'.

Edward the Bruce, a kinsman of the O'Neills (descendants of the Uí Néill), had spent a good deal of his childhood in Ulster and entertained high hopes that the Irish would arise in his favour. The reality was infinitely more complex, not least because so many Irish clans were already locked into a bitter internecine war. As such, the younger Bruce became just another player in this game of thrones, albeit one of the most powerful.

He quickly secured control of much of Ulster and began styling himself 'Edward, by the grace of God, king of Ireland'. Many Ulster lords swore fealty to him, although most were clearly hedging their bets. The Scots then powered south, destroying towns and settlements across Leinster and brutally putting all in their path to the sword. They were soon as despised as the English, a reputation not improved by a run of severe winters that led to a famine of such intensity that, according to the Annals of Ulster, 'people undoubtedly used to eat each other throughout Ireland'.

By 1317, the English had regained their composure and Edward the Bruce came under mounting pressure, despite the brief support of his brother, King Robert, and a large army of gallowglass mercenaries from the Hebrides. His morale was not helped when, despite a costly PR campaign, the Pope refused to accept his claim to the Irish throne.

Everything came to a head on 14 October 1318 when Bruce's army was overwhelmed by a superior English force at the Hill of Faughart near Dundalk. At least thirty Scottish knights perished, including Edward the Bruce, thus ending the grandiose dreams of a Gaelic brotherhood. The Annals of Ulster lambasted Bruce as 'the destroyer of Ireland' and applauded his death as the best 'deed' since time began. The fallen king's head was sent to Edward II, while his body was divided into four quarters. Part of his remains were said to have been buried at Faughart beneath a large flat stone that can still be seen today.

14 Prince Lionel Comes to Carlow

 Just two towers and a crumbling curtain wall are all that survive of Carlow Castle but 650 years ago this limestone bastion was the administrative headquarters of English rule in Ireland, presided over by Prince Lionel of Antwerp, third son of Edward III, King of England and Lord of Ireland.

There has been a castle at Carlow since 1181 when the first Anglo-Norman settlers built a motte and bailey on an elevated rise at the very point where the River Burren enters the River Barrow, with a marshland to the east. The location was defensively sound and economically smart, given the castle's proximity to a navigable river system, a vital factor in medieval trade. In due course, the property passed to William Marshal, Lord of Leinster, who swept the timbers aside and replaced them with a mighty new stone fortress.

Completed in about 1213, Carlow's central keep rose 20 m (70 ft) high and was flanked by four drum towers, each perfectly

looped for crossbow archers to shower their deadly arrows upon any would-be invaders. The design was almost certainly inspired by the castles in Normandy that Marshal knew in his youth. The Great Hall, which occupied the bulk of the first floor, was where Marshal and his seneschal (the castle steward) hosted assemblies of vassals and tenants on Christian feast days, as well as important judicial and fiscal occasions. The main bedrooms were in the towers, at least three of which had en-suite garderobes (lavatories). One of the surviving towers served as a prison, while two of the other towers also held a kitchen and an exchequer.

The castle subsequently passed to Marshal's grandson Roger Bigod, 4th Earl of Norfolk. His son, the 5th Earl, came to Carlow in 1279, in part to lock up a seneschal who had been swindling him but also to make his peace with the increasingly aggressive Mac-Murrough clan, descendants of Dermot, the king of Leinster, who had so fatefully invited the Normans to Ireland a century earlier. Lord Norfolk, who could also claim descent from King Dermot, met with the MacMurroughs and, via a combination of his charm and money, along with plenty of wine and some fine furs for their ladies, convinced them to back down.

Between 1283 and 1292, Lord Norfolk embarked upon an extensive restoration of Carlow Castle, shipping twelve thousand wooden shingles up the Barrow from the Dunleckney woods to re-cover the roof of the Great Hall. The four towers were also refurbished, especially the Exchequer House, which had a treasurer's office and court at ground level, with a saferoom upstairs for the wooden chests that held all the money and records. With Norfolk's support, Carlow evolved into a prosperous market town, trading with other towns along the Barrow, while the lordship at large also enjoyed an economic boom. When Norfolk died childless, the castle was left to the Crown.

So it was that Carlow became the castle of choice for Lionel of Antwerp, second surviving son of Edward III, who served as governor of Ireland from 1361 until 1367. Named after the Flemish city of his birth, the King's son was twenty-three years old when he arrived in Carlow. As a boy he was married to Elizabeth de Burgh, sole heiress of the Earl of Ulster. In 1347, while the Black Death ripped Europe apart, young Lionel was created Earl of Ulster. He was elevated to the Duchy of Clarence soon after he took up office in Ireland.

Lionel's brief was to halt the degeneration of the lordship of Ireland, which, among other things, had led to a sharp decline in revenue for the Crown. This was largely blamed on the miscellaneous Norman and English settlers having adopted Irish law, customs, costume and language to such an extent that they had, in the words of the 17th-century historian John Lynch, become *Hiberniores Hibernis ipsis*, meaning 'more Irish than the Irish themselves'.

Alarmed by an early defeat of his army by the O'Byrne sept, who predominated in the Wicklow Mountains, Prince Lionel decided to relocate the Exchequer from Dublin to Carlow Castle. Accessible by both river and road, it was deemed more convenient than Dublin for most treasury officials. Further improvements were made to the towers, including the Exchequer House, as well as the Great Hall and the walls. The interior was also revamped and this was probably the period when the roof was raised and a second floor installed, thereby creating further rooms for the Exchequer's staff.

In 1362, Lionel piled more administrative responsibility on Carlow when he moved the Court of Common Pleas (or Common Bench), which dealt with civil cases, south from Dublin and placed it in a new purpose-built house alongside the castle.

The castle was now home to a sheriff, two lawyers and a chief serjeant, as well as numerous money collectors, clerks and other personnel. It was defended by a garrison that is thought to have comprised of little more than the constable, a man-at-arms and eight archers.

Lionel had set aside a large budget to wall the entire town, a project destined to drag on for many long years after his departure. In the absence of such a wall, Carlow Castle was by no means secure. In 1363, both the Exchequer and the Court fled back to Dublin because the town was under constant attack. However, by 1364, both were firmly ensconced in Carlow once more and they would remain in the castle for the next thirty years.

In 1366, Lionel summoned a meeting of the Irish Parliament in Kilkenny Castle, 35 km (22 miles) southwest of Carlow, at which the Statutes of Kilkenny were passed. This was a series of thirty-five acts designed to curb the settlers' enthusiasm for 'going native', including prohibitions on the use of Irish language and dress, and Irish names within the colony; intermarriage with the native Irish; the playing of hurling; and the employment of Irish minstrels, harpers or bards. Most of this was simply reiterating existing laws, excluding the 'new' bans on language and minstrels, but the statutes were largely ignored as unenforceable claptrap. For instance, the demand that 'every Englishman use the English language' was widely ridiculed because the statutes themselves were written in French.

Lacking sufficient resources to implement the statutes, Lionel abandoned Ireland in a huff the following year. In 1368, the widowed prince was married again in Italy, amid lavish festivities, to a daughter of the sadistic Milanese ruler, Galeazzo II Visconti. Some months later, the twenty-nine-year-old prince was taken ill at Alba and died. His father-in-law is rumoured to have poisoned him. Upon Lionel's death, his son-in-law Edmund Mortimer, 3rd Earl of March – husband of his only child, Philippa – became Earl of Ulster and Earl Marshal of England. Edmund and Philippa were the ancestors of the principal claimants of the House of York in the Wars of the Roses.

Both the Exchequer and the Court of Common Bench returned to Dublin in 1394, the year in which Richard II, king of England and a nephew of Lionel, sailed to Ireland with the largest force yet brought to the island. The aim of King Richard's eight thousand soldiers was to annihilate the army of Art Mór MacMurrough, king of Leinster, who had risen up against English rule, partly in response to the Statutes of Kilkenny. A temporary truce was followed by a renewal of the war a few years later when Roger Mortimer, 4th Earl of March and Richard II's designated heir, was killed in a skirmish at Kellistown, 10 km (6 miles) southeast of Carlow Castle.

In 1399, Richard II returned to Ireland with three thousand men, including three dukes, three earls and all five captains of his bodyguard. It was assumed that his mission was to avenge his cousin's death but there is a theory that he planned to crown his own nephew Thomas Holland – one of the three dukes – as king of Ireland. In any event, the mission was aborted and Richard was destined to be overthrown by Henry Bolingbroke, subsequently Henry IV, later that year. He died in captivity in 1400.

Over the ensuing centuries, Carlow Castle passed through a series of families, including the O'Brien dynasty, whose patriarch, the Great Earl of Thomond, considerably restored the building in the early 17th century. It survived two sieges in the 1640s and an artillery bombardment by Henry Ireton, Oliver Cromwell's son-in-law. The Cromwellian army then demolished much of the castle's interior, knocking out the windows, doors and floors in order to ensure it would never again be used for defensive purposes.

And so it remained, abandoned and unloved, until 1814 when a mysterious English doctor called Philip Parry Price Middleton (or Myddelton) acquired the building. He planned to convert Carlow Castle into a private Maison de Santé, or lunatic asylum, as psychiatric institutions were then known. It's arguable that he should have been its first inmate because he ended up blowing the six-hundred-year-old castle into smithereens. He was either trying to create a new entrance or to pierce new windows into the old thick walls. In any event, he opted to use dynamite blasting powder for the job. The explosives weakened the entire structure to such an extent that the two eastern towers promptly collapsed, along with three-quarters of the adjoining walls. Amazingly, not a sinner was hurt.

15 Great Pretenders & Warring Roses

In the late 15th century, the lordship of Ireland was inevitably dragged into the Wars of the Roses, a thirty-year-long civil war that raged between supporters of rival claimants to the English throne. In Ireland, the Butler family, headed by the Earl of Ormonde, lined out for the House of Lancaster, while the family's bitter foes, the FitzGeralds, led by the earls of Desmond and Kildare, were staunch allies of the House of York. The island also served as a supply base for troops, as well as a place of sanctuary for English nobles on the run.

In 1462, the wars ripped into Ireland when soldiers loyal to Thomas FitzGerald, 7th Earl of Desmond, annihilated the Butlers, killing upwards of four hundred men with sword, mace and axe, in a brutal day-long pitched battle at Piltown in southern County Kilkenny. In Irish, Piltown is called Baile an Phuill, the 'town of the blood', a nod to that day in which the blood of dead and dying Butlers seeped into the River Suir. The Butlers were still reeling from the death of their chief, James Butler, 5th Earl of Ormonde, who was beheaded at Newcastle in 1461 following the Battle of Towton, probably the bloodiest battle ever fought on British soil. The victor at Towton was eighteen-year-old Edward, Duke of York, who promptly deposed Henry VI, the Lancastrian king, and ascended the throne as Edward IV. Meanwhile, Lord Ormonde's head was among those set upon London Bridge for all to see.

John Butler, younger brother of James, succeeded as 6th Earl but was attainted for supporting the Lancastrians. He was not present at Piltown; by the time Lord Desmond's troops swept into Kilkenny and plundered the city after the battle, John was sagely en route to seven years of exile in Portugal and France. A brilliant linguist, he was pardoned by Edward IV, who declared him 'the goodliest knight he ever beheld and the first gentleman in Christendom', adding that 'if good breeding and liberal qualities were lost in the world, they might be all found in the Earl of Ormond'. In 1475, John was restored to his Irish lands and titles but he never returned to take them up; he reputedly died on pilgrimage to the Holy Land two years later.

Although unmarried, the 6th Earl of Ormonde had at least three illegitimate sons with Reynalda O'Brien, a daughter of the king of Thomond. The eldest was Sir James Dubh Butler (aka Black James) who was one of the principal players in suppressing Perkin Warbeck's bid for the English kingdom. Warbeck, a Flemish peasant, claimed to be one of the 'Princes in the Tower' supposedly murdered by Richard III. The 9th Earl of Desmond, a son of the champion of Piltown, was his main backer, along with John Walters, the mayor of Cork, and many other leading Cork citizens, some of whom had helped teach Warbeck how to speak English. Warbeck's rebellion fell apart when he failed to capture Waterford, for which the city was later given its motto, *Urbs Intacta Manet Waterfordia*, meaning 'Waterford remains the untaken city'.

Lord Desmond managed to make his peace with Henry VII who, in return for the Earl's loyalty, granted him the customs of the southern ports of Youghal, Cork, Kinsale, Baltimore and Limerick. However, there was no such joy for Warbeck and Walters, who were executed in London in 1499. Cork's city charter was temporarily forfeited as a reprimand; Cork became known as the Rebel City ever after.

At the time of Warbeck's rebellion, the most powerful man in Ireland was Gerard Mór FitzGerald, the ultra-shrewd Earl of Kildare, who held the office of Lord Deputy of Ireland for nearly forty years. Henry VII was understandably wary of Kildare, who had personally crowned Lambert Simnel, another ill-fated pretender to the throne, in Dublin in 1487; Kildare's brother died fighting for Simnel. After Warbeck's coup, Henry VII dismissed Kildare from his post as Lord Deputy and dispatched him to the Tower of London. In response, Kildare's younger brother seized Carlow Castle – a Crown property – and mounted the FitzGeralds' banner from its battlements. James Dubh Butler duly besieged and recaptured the castle, triggering fresh rivalry with the FitzGeralds.

Peace between the houses was memorably restored when James Dubh and Lord Kildare shook hands through a hole cut in the chapter house door of St Patrick's Cathedral, thus giving rise to the expression 'to chance one's arm'. The 'Door of Reconciliation', as it became known, is on exhibition in the cathedral to this day. Kildare later persuaded the King that he was an innocent man, stitched up by 'false knaves'. The exasperated Tudor monarch reinstated him as Lord Deputy, declaring that 'if all Ireland cannot rule this man, let him rule all Ireland'. As for James Dubh, he was murdered by his cousin Red Piers, later the 8th Earl of Ormonde, in 1497.

Following the death of the 6th Earl of Ormonde in 1477, another brother Thomas succeeded as 7th Earl. Thomas had done much to restore the Butlers' credibility after the Piltown debacle when he captured four Desmond ships, 'with all they contained', which is said to have instantly restored the Butlers' fortunes. Knighted at the coronation of Richard III, for whom he served as a privy councillor, he also became a close friend of Henry VII, the ultimate victor of the Wars of the Roses, who restored him to his estates in 1485.

The 7th Earl of Ormonde was known as 'the Wool Earl' on account of his enormous wealth, which included seventy-two manors in England. These had been part of a terrific dowry that came his way when he married the heiress Anne Hankford. He served as Lord Chamberlain to Henry VII's queen, Elizabeth of York, as well as to Henry VIII's first wife, Catherine of Aragon. When he died in 1515, he bequeathed an ancient gold and ivory drinking horn to his namesake and grandson, Thomas Boleyn. In 1529, Boleyn himself was created Earl of Ormonde, in part because his daughter Anne had caught the King's eye, setting in motion the high drama of the Reformation. It is sometimes claimed that Anne Boleyn was born at Ormonde Castle in Carrick-on-Suir, County Tipperary, but that sadly appears to be an unprovable fantasy. Anne's actual birthplace is unknown but her siblings were born at Blickling in Norfolk and she grew up at Hever Castle in Kent.

16 The Midland Shires

Thrice three hundred and three score,
Tale unheard by thee before,
Feasted free in Calvagh's hall,
Caring light what might befall.

 On the day that Mary Tudor ascended the throne as queen of England and Ireland in 1553, most of present-day County Offaly and parts of County Westmeath formed a territory known as Feara Ceall, or Firceall. By the end of her reign five years later, the entire area had been shired as part of the first wave of English plantations in Ireland. 'Firceall' translates as 'men of the churches', a reference to the large number of abbeys, friaries and monasteries in this once forested landscape.

Since 839, the region had been the dominion of the O'Molloy family, princes of Firceall, who claimed descent from Niall of the Nine Hostages, a quasi-legendary 4th-century-AD monarch. 'O'Molloy's Country' was a wild and reckless landscape where trust was a rare commodity. Many princes were slain by their own flesh and blood in the brutal inheritance contests that arose under the Irish law of tanistry, the system for passing on titles and lands. As well as internecine conflicts, the family was often at war with neighbouring septs such as the O'Carrolls of Ely, the MacCoughlans of Delvin Ethra and the O'Connors of Offaly.

In 1556, Queen Mary appointed a brilliant young courtier named Sir Henry Sidney to the office of Lord Justice of Ireland. He successfully introduced an act into the Irish Parliament that formally created King's County (now County Offaly) – named for King Philip II of Spain, the husband, or consort, of Queen Mary – from the combined territories of the O'Connor Faly and Ely O'Carroll families. Queen's County (now County Laois), named for Queen Mary, was also created out of the former O'More lands in Leix and Offaly. Daingean, the new capital of King's County, was renamed Philipstown after the Spanish monarch; he would become England's greatest enemy when he launched his ill-fated Armada twenty-two years later. The fort

at Leix, hitherto known as Fort Protector, became the capital of the new Queen's County and was renamed Maryborough (now Portlaoise).

The new shire of King's County included Firceall, which, unsurprisingly, made the O'Molloys profoundly unhappy. However, when the reigning prince kicked up, Sidney 'directed his colours' against the clan, marched into the country, burned down most of their buildings and installed a new prince who was game on to swear immediate allegiance to Queen Mary.

The pioneering plantation scheme that followed the shiring of the Midlands called for two-thirds of the natives' lands to be expropriated and allocated to 'Englishmen born in England or Ireland'. However, despite the arrival of many ambitious new settlers, including the Moores (later earls of Drogheda), the

plantation was a limited success. Constant resistance from the O'Molloys and other neighbouring clans continued throughout the century, leading to frequent incursions by the Tudor army from Dublin. As late as 1575, Sidney himself was expressing grave misgivings and bemoaning the costs of trying to sustain the venture.

In 1580, forty-four-year-old Lord Grey de Wilton was dispatched to Ireland as the new Lord Deputy with a force of six thousand men. His central task was to halt a new offensive that Gerald FitzGerald, 15th Earl of Desmond, had launched against the English planters in Munster. The rebellion had already begun to spill out of Munster by the time Lord Grey arrived but disaster ensued when possibly as many as eight hundred of his soldiers were ambushed and killed at Glenmalure in the Wicklow Mountains (see also chapter 17). With renewed steeliness, and reinforcements of 150 cavalry and 6 infantry companies from England, Lord Grey went on the warpath. In the process, he completely overran the Midlands, including Firceall, and executed Hugh O'Molloy, Prince of Firceall, for being 'a seditious person'.

Conall, the next O'Molloy prince, opted to toe the Tudor line, surrendering his lands to Queen Elizabeth I and receiving them as a re-grant by a patent dated 1590. In return for his loyalty, he was appointed hereditary royal standard-bearer of Leinster (an office largely exercised within the Pale) and granted an official coat of arms. In 1595, he was invited to carry the Queen's Standard alongside the Tudor army that marched north from Dublin to confront the Ulster chieftains who were in open revolt against the English garrisons in Ulster.

When Conall died in the spring of 1599, his son Calvagh (or Caolbach) assumed his place in Parliament 'by the power of the Queen'. Inevitably, other family members objected and a new succession crisis ensued. This coincided with the arrival of Hugh O'Neill's rebel army from Ulster into Firceall in 1600. O'Neill was seeking vengeance for the massacre of a company of his mercenaries by the Ely O'Carrolls. He and his men stayed as guests of Calvagh for nine days, during which time they plundered the Ely O'Carrolls. Providing such hospitality to one of the Crown's principal enemies went down poorly with the Dublin authorities, who ordered the O'Carrolls to pulverize Firceall with 'fire and sword' the moment O'Neill's army had left.

It was not all grim; even while the Nine Years War was in motion, the Irish-speaking Calvagh hosted 'nine hundred and sixty persons' to a party at his castle 'for the feast of Christmas' and 'entertained them there for the space of twelve days'. Sadly, the specific details of what they ate or drank or how they entertained themselves are not recorded, but this is the only known party of its size held in Ireland during that period.

Calvagh was refused admission to King James's Parliament of 1613 on the basis that he could not speak English. That same year, the authorities in Dublin granted a large portion of his lands to Francis Blundell, a surveyor from Bedfordshire who had risen to become Clerk of the Commissioners for Defective Titles. Other O'Molloy estates were simultaneously awarded to the Earl of Kildare. The O'Molloys protested, of course, and many were to die over the course of the 17th century vainly trying to turn back time and undo all the legal paperwork that had somehow tied them in knots and deprived them of the lands that they had considered theirs for nearly eight hundred years.

17 Sir William Stanley, Public Enemy No. 1

In 1588, Philip II of Spain sent a fleet of 130 ships to destroy the Protestant realm of his former sister-in-law, Elizabeth I, queen of England and Ireland. As the Spanish Armada set sail, at least one of Philip's advisors predicted a disaster; William Stanley had been among the most respected commanders in the Elizabethan army until his shock decision to change sides and join the Spanish.

Born in 1548, William was the eldest son of Sir Rowland Stanley who, at ninety-six, was the oldest knight in England when he died in 1614. William's mother was the daughter of a prosperous Chester merchant and the widow of Henry, Lord de Bunbury, an ancestor of mine. The youngster was raised a Catholic and educated under the patronage of his kinsman, Edward Stanley, 3rd Earl of Derby. At the age of twelve, he married ten-year-old Ann Dutton; their marriage was later dissolved. Like most teenage boys of his rank, he sought a military career and, in 1567, he sailed for the Netherlands – then largely under the

control of Catholic Spain – where he served under the tyrannical Duke of Alba.

In 1570, the twenty-two-year-old arrived in Ireland where he was to serve for the next fifteen years alongside men such as Sir Walter Raleigh, Sir Humphrey Gilbert and the poet Edmund Spenser. Stanley came to the fore during the 15th Earl of Desmond's rebellion of 1579–83 when, despite his adherence to the Catholic faith, he proved to be among the most proactive officers in the Tudor army. Many Irishmen felt comfortable serving in his ranks precisely because he was a Catholic. His leadership skills were exceptional and his magnetic charm enabled him to become one of the greatest recruiters of his day.

In Munster, his men 'burned and spoiled the countrie, and put to the sword whomsoever they thought good'. He secured much of County Limerick for the Crown, capturing the Desmond stronghold of Adare and commanding the cavalry that chased the Irish from the field of battle at nearby Manister. He wrestled control of the mighty Desmond castle of Castlemaine that guarded the entrance to the Dingle Peninsula in County Kerry. For these 'gallantries', he was knighted in Waterford by Sir William Drury, Lord Justice of Ireland.

When the Wicklow chieftain Feagh McHugh O'Byrne hammered the Tudor army at Glenmalure in 1580, Stanley was ordered to defend the Pale against further attacks. He became notorious as a rebel hunter, from the Wicklow Mountains all the way south to the Blackwater Valley. He burned the O'Byrnes' headquarters at Ballinacor and slaughtered scores of their Kavanagh and O'Toole allies, earning high praise from the Elizabethan elite in Dublin.

By 1584, Stanley had been appointed commander of Lismore Castle in County Waterford but his hopes to be made president of Connaught were thwarted. Instead he was appointed sheriff of Cork, in which capacity he claimed to have hanged three hundred rebels and left the rest of Cork so petrified that, as he put it, 'a man might now travel the whole country and none molest him'. At the end of 1584, Stanley was sent to Antrim to confront the Ulster rebel Sorley Boy MacDonnell. However, he was ambushed near Ballycastle and so severely wounded that he had to return to England where he was given a hero's welcome.

Meanwhile, Lord Desmond was betrayed and captured in a forest near Tralee; his severed head, 'pickled in a pipkin', was sent to rot on London Bridge as a warning to aspiring traitors. About 200,000 hectares (500,000 acres) of Munster were seized from Desmond's heirs and allies, annexed to the English Crown and carved up by Elizabeth's Privy Council as part of a major new plantation scheme. The richest and most fertile lands were divided into twenty-three blocks (seigniories) of approximately 4,800 hectares (12,000 acres) each, 'not accounting mountains, bogs, or barren heath'.

Stanley may have been a Catholic but his first loyalty had always been to the Crown, irrespective of religion. As such, he had good cause to anticipate a share of the spoils. However, much to his disappointment, his service was ignored during this massive land redistribution. His comrade Raleigh secured three seigniories, giving him an estate of over 17,000 hectares (42,000 acres), and went on to become mayor of Youghal in County Cork. Many others who served on the fringes were also handsomely rewarded.

Stanley was still smarting at this snub when the Queen ordered him to help one of her favourites, the Earl of Leicester, oust the Spanish from the Netherlands. Upon receiving this command, he journeyed to Ireland and amassed a regiment of twelve hundred troops, mainly Catholic pikemen. There are reasonable grounds to suspect that he had, in fact, recruited this Irish force to assist in a major plot to assassinate Elizabeth and install her Catholic cousin Mary, Queen of Scots, on the English throne. Known as the Babington Plot, this conspiracy was apparently hatched by the Spanish in cahoots with Catholic Jesuits in England. People would later swear that they had seen Sir William in deep conversation with various Jesuit priests. He was certainly communicating with Bernardino de Mendoza, the former Spanish ambassador to England who had been expelled from the country for his involvement in a similar plot to murder Elizabeth.

Stanley kept his Irish regiment on standby while he awaited the outcome of the Babington Plot. Upon hearing of its failure, he made haste for the Netherlands where he led his pikemen into action at Zutphen, the battle in which the dashing Elizabethan poet Sir Philip Sidney – regarded as the Byron of his day – was fatally wounded. Stanley fought with such passion that Leicester declared him 'worth his weight in pearls'. He went on to help the English army capture Deventer, regarded as the most important town in the Netherlands after Antwerp and Amsterdam. Widely hailed for his heroism across Protestant Europe, Stanley was appointed governor of Deventer in the autumn of 1586. His own troops were assigned to garrison the harbour town.

Then, just months later, Stanley stunned everybody by handing Deventer back to the Spanish. He is assumed to have committed this brazen treachery in direct response to the Elizabethan government's failure to give him either land or high office in Ireland. As such, he must have kicked himself when, soon afterwards, he learned that the Queen had personally proposed him as a new viceroy of Ireland shortly before his betrayal.

Declared an outlaw, Stanley journeyed to the Spanish court where he was soon offering advice to Philip II on how best to invade England. He specifically recommended using Ireland as a launch pad. Not only did he have extensive personal, logistical and geographical knowledge of the island but he was also confident that the Catholic Irish would arise in support of Spain. His advice was ignored and Philip II instead dispatched the Armada to invade England directly. It transpired to be one of the greatest disasters in Spanish history.

By 1590, Stanley was commanding the English Legion, a force of a thousand Irish and English Catholic soldiers whom he led into action against Dutch Protestants and French Huguenots over the ensuing years. He is also understood to have been behind at least four abortive plots to assassinate Elizabeth. The conspirators included Patrick O'Collun and Hugh Cahill, two Irishmen from Stanley's regiment. Among Stanley's officers were Guy Fawkes and Tom Wintour, two of the key figures in the Gunpowder Plot of 1605. In the wake of that botched conspiracy, Stanley was placed under house arrest in Brussels but it is not clear how involved he actually was; he was quick to cover his tracks from the moment it failed. In their tortured confessions, Fawkes claimed Stanley was involved but Wintour insisted he knew nothing.

One theory holds that Stanley provided vital information to Sir Robert Cecil, the Secretary of State, in return for a pardon from the Crown. If so, it paid off because in 1606 Cecil exonerated him from the charge although he was still exiled from England. Upon his release, he held a public thanksgiving at St Rumbold's Cathedral in the Flemish city of Mechelen. At this point, he seems to have accepted that the restoration of Catholic power in England was a lost cause. He became a recluse for the remainder of his long life, helping to establish a Jesuit novitiate in Liège in 1614. He was never allowed to return to England but lived his final years with the English Carthusians in Ostend. He died at Ghent in 1630 and was buried at Mechelen.

18 Rise & Fall: The Maguires of Fermanagh

 In a quiet field above the County Fermanagh town of Lisnaskea stands an ancient mound, almost certainly a Neolithic burial tomb, known locally as the Moat Ring, or Sciath Gabhra in Irish. This is the spot where fifteen men were crowned as kings of Fermanagh between 1264 and 1589, all belonging to the Maguire family, once among the most prominent dynasties in the northwest of Ireland.

By the standards of most Irish kings, and indeed of many European kings, the Maguires boasted a remarkably serene track record. Their reigns averaged over two decades each, with many notching up more than forty years, while challenges to the throne were rare and only one of the fifteen was assassinated. Occasionally they were obliged to arm and defend themselves against the O'Neills, the O'Donnells and other families, or to resolve internal squabbles, and some Maguires were wont to invade neighbouring lands. However, in general, Fermanagh under the Maguires was a stable place for nearly three centuries.

The Maguires were exceptionally progressive, their households replete with historians, poets and learned men. They were also tremendous benefactors of the Christian church, introducing new orders, endowing churches and embarking on pilgrimages to Rome and Santiago de Compostela in Spain. In their twilight, many retired in good time to prepare for their death.

The family descend from Donn Mór Maguire, a warrior who witnessed attempts by King John's government in Dublin to build castles at Clones, County Monaghan, Belturbet, County Cavan, and Belleek, County Fermanagh, in the early 13th century. Donn Mór also lived to see all three castles destroyed by the indigenous Irish. In 1264, his son Donn Carrach Maguire was the first of the line to be crowned king of Fermanagh. Hailed by the bards as 'Ireland's Most Generous Lord', he lived at Lisnaskea

and reigned for forty-two-years until 1301 when, as the Annals of Ulster recorded, he 'rested in Christ'.

Donn's descendants continued to expand the Maguires' territory, albeit as a subservient family to the O'Donnell of Tyrconnell dynasty, which was, for the most part, subservient to O'Neill of Tyrone. Among the most influential of the Maguires was Philip of the Battle Axe, who reigned from 1363 to 1395. He earned his moniker by fending off attacks by rival MacMahon, O'Neill and O'Connor chieftains in a series of gruesome battles. Fermanagh essentially took on the county's present shape and size on his watch when he established it as a buffer kingdom between the warring realms of Ulster and Connaught. His greatest asset was a fleet of white sail boats on Lough Erne that gave him mastery of the waters. At one point, his fleet sailed into

Lough Oughter in County Cavan and captured the O'Reilly chief who subsequently became his foremost ally.

Hugh the Hospitable, Philip's son, built the original castles at Enniskillen and Monea and was widely applauded for his virtue and munificence. Once a year, he would seat himself beneath a whitethorn tree at Monea at sunrise, from where he would receive his extended family and neighbours, listening to their woes, dispensing wise counsel and handing out dowries to girls whose fathers were in financial difficulty. A frequent pilgrim to Rome, Spain and Italy, he was returning from the Holy Land when he died in Kinsale, County Cork, in 1428.

Hugh's successor, Thomas the Younger, was considerably less pious. He once decorated his garden with the heads of sixteen O'Rourke nobles whom his men had slain during a raid on their strongholds at Bawnboy and Ballyconnell. Thomas's descendants were the senior, or 'Lisnaskea', branch of the Maguires while those of his brother Philip became the junior, or 'Enniskillen', branch. These two branches evolved into increasingly bitter foes as the crown passed from one to the other over the ensuing century.

By 1500, the family owned almost all of the present county of Fermanagh and manned all the principal positions; the bishops, archdeacons, priors and parish priests were all Maguires, while most other families kowtowed to them. The Maguires' loyalty swung between the O'Neill and O'Donnell families, as those two warring dynasties vied for supreme power in northwest Ireland.

In the late 16th century, such self-contained political disputes were completely trumped by the arrival of a new force in the region, namely the Tudor army of Queen Elizabeth I. This coincided with the reign of Cuchonnacht II, one of the most scholarly Maguire chiefs, who acceded to a request to surrender his lands to the Queen in 1585; he received them back without the church lands. When the Tudor administration in Dublin formally shired Fermanagh the following year, Cuchonnacht must have known the end was nigh. The Tudors had already seized most of Munster and, in 1585, they effectively took control of Connaught. Almost all of Ireland was now under the control of the Crown and its allies, bar certain pockets of Ulster.

It fell to Cuchonnacht's son and heir Hugh (Aodh) to defend his ancestral kingdom. In 1589, this fearless young man stepped down from the coronation stone at Lisnaskea as the 15th Maguire chief of Fermanagh. He realized that his late father's conciliatory attitude to the Tudors was a ticket to nowhere. Loyalty to the Crown clearly counted for little: the teenaged Red Hugh O'Donnell, whose father had been a loyal supporter of the Crown, was banged up in Dublin Castle for four years. Hugh Rua MacMahon, Lord of Monaghan, had briefly tried his hand at friendship with the Tudors; when his help was no longer required, they charged him with treason and had him hanged on a tree outside his own front door.

Initially, Hugh Maguire played the game, accepting a knighthood in Christ Church Cathedral in 1591. The following year, however, he helped Red Hugh, his cousin, break out of Dublin Castle. Both men now perceived that the Tudors posed an existential threat to their world and gradually they persuaded the region's most powerful noble, Hugh O'Neill, Earl of Tyrone – who was raised in Queen Elizabeth's court – that he must come on board.

As the Nine Years War began, so Ulster became a battleground between the warring armies of Protestant England and Catholic Ireland. At first, Maguire and his allies managed to push the English out of Fermanagh but reinforcements returned, capturing both Enniskillen and Lisnaskea and installing a string of garrisons from Newry in the northeast of Ireland all the way to Ballyshannon in the northwest, including Monaghan, Benburb and Lisnaskea.

The Irish enjoyed some exceptional successes, not least when O'Neill's great victory at the Battle of the Yellow Ford gave him complete power in Ulster in 1598. However, when their armies moved south, the campaign began to flounder. In 1600, Hugh Maguire led his men as far south as Cork, where he rashly decided to raid an English camp; he completely underestimated his opponents who overwhelmed them, killing thirty-two Maguires, including Hugh, his son, his foster-father and his chaplain. Legend holds that Hugh's horse refused to eat after his death and withered away. Hugh Maguire was buried alongside his ancestor and namesake, Hugh the Hospitable, founder of Enniskillen, who had been buried in Cork 172 years earlier.

The loss of Hugh Maguire was an enormous blow to the Gaelic alliance, not least when a power struggle among his heirs saw one claimant form a treacherous pact with the Tudors that paved the way for an English conquest of the region. This came just as O'Neill and O'Donnell saw their dreams shattered by an absolute English victory over their combined forces at Kinsale.

Hugh Maguire's brother Cuchonnacht Og (Constantine) is considered the last Maguire king of Fermanagh, although he was never crowned. He returned from the defeat at Kinsale to find his lands devastated by the English conquerors. By 1605, over half of his estate had been seized and parcelled out to planters. The following year he purchased a vessel in Rouen, dolled it up as an innocuous fishing boat and sailed it back to Lough Swilly in County Donegal. In September 1607, approximately one hundred passengers boarded Cuchonnacht's ship at Rathmullan.

The ship duly sailed for France with the cream of Ireland's Gaelic nobility in what became known as the Flight of the Earls.

Having reached Quillebeuf in Normandy, most passengers went overland to Rome to meet the Pope. Cuchonnacht was among those who reached Rome but, always restless, he was determined to convince the Spanish king to send a new armada to Ireland. In the summer of 1608, he joined forces with James MacMahon and boarded a ship at Naples that was bound for Spain. While staying a night at Ostia, both men became violently ill with fever and died. They were buried at a Franciscan monastery near Genoa.

The remaining Maguire lands in Ireland were subsequently vested in Cuchonnacht's kinsman Bryan, who was created Baron Maguire of Enniskillen in 1627. Bryan sponsored the celebrated Annals of the Four Masters, but his successors were fated for a sticky end. His son Connor, the 2nd Baron, was hanged, drawn and quartered in London for high treason after the Irish Rebellion in 1641, while his brother, Colonel Rory Maguire, was killed in a skirmish in 1648. Over the next century, the titular Barons Maguire of Enniskillen served in the Jacobite and French armies, with the last one serving as a captain in the Comte de Lally's regiment of Irish infantry.

19 Cromwell's Tailor

In August 1649, Oliver Cromwell, the most powerful figure in the new Commonwealth of England, stepped ashore at Ringsend in Dublin to commence a nine-month military campaign that would earn him immortality as the most despised human in Irish history. His mission was to annihilate the Confederation, an alliance of Irish Catholic nobles, gentry and clergymen who had pledged allegiance to the deposed House of Stuart. The execution of King Charles, the Stuart king, in January 1649 had hardened the Confederation's resolve and, despite bubbling internal divisions, the Kilkenny-based alliance had secured control of nearly all of Ireland by the close of July. The glaring exception was Dublin, to which city the Confederate army now marched. And then they blew it.

Credit must be given to Michael Jones, the commander of Dublin's pro-Cromwell or Parliamentarian garrison, who launched a surprise attack on the incoming forces while they were at rest in Rathmines. Thousands of Confederates were killed or captured while Jones also nabbed their artillery and supplies. The Bleeding Horse, a venerable pub on Dublin's Camden Street, was reputedly named for a wounded horse that stumbled into the tavern in the wake of the battle.

Jones's victory was a game-changer from which the Confederation never recovered. Understandably, Cromwell regarded it as 'an astonishing mercy, so great and seasonable that we are like them that dreamed'. Within two weeks, the fifty-year-old Cromwell had arrived in Dublin with a fleet of thirty-five ships laden with artillery and three thousand battle-hardened troops. His son-in-law Henry Ireton followed two days later with a further seventy-seven ships.

The ensuing campaign is remembered for its brutality, particularly in the port towns of Drogheda and Wexford where Cromwell's Ironsides ruthlessly put the defeated garrisons to the sword. Still greater calamity followed with a widespread famine and an outbreak of bubonic plague. By the time the last Confederates submitted in Cavan in 1653, it is estimated that between 20 and 40 per cent of Ireland's pre-war population of 1.5 million had perished.

And yet there is always someone who can turn a war to their advantage. Step forward Daniel O'Byrne, a Catholic tailor based beside Christ Church Cathedral on Dublin's Winetavern Street. He is believed to have been a grandson of Sir Phelim O'Byrne whose father Feagh McHugh O'Byrne, Lord of Ranelagh, was the arch-nemesis of Queen Elizabeth's Tudor generals for many long years. While Daniel's uncles were leading lights in the Confederacy, he played a more prudent hand. According to his kinsman, Garrett Byrne of Fallowbeg: 'This Daniel...was bred up in the business of a clothier, and afterwards carried on the trade of a tailor, and kept forty men constantly working at that business. He used to buy all the white cloth in Dublin, get it coloured red, and clothe forty thousand men with the same for General Cromwell, and never call for money until all was finished, and then received drafts from Cromwell on the Treasury, where he got cash, for which he purchased estates.'

Garrett Byrne's figure of 40,000 is remarkably precise; modern historians believe that about 43,000 English soldiers served with Cromwell's New Model Army in Ireland, as well as 9,000 Irish Protestants. Red coats were indeed standard dress for Cromwell's infantry, the colour having been officially adopted in 1645. The choice of the earthy red was simply because its 'Venetian Red' pigment was the cheapest and most widely available at the time. However, the fashion stuck and over the next 250 years, the 'redcoats' of British soldiers would become one of the most emblematic sights of the British Empire.

Daniel Byrne pumped much of his tailor's fortune into buying a large chunk of the Queen's County. He reputedly paid Sir Walter Whelan a sum of £150,000 for the Timogue and Morett estates, near Timahoe, comprising fifteen townlands. The Deed, signed by both Daniel Byrne and Oliver Cromwell, survives among the Marchioness of Lansdowne's 'Irish Estate' papers at Bowood House in Wiltshire, England.

A still juicier acquisition came when he secured ownership of the lordship of Shean near the Great Heath of Maryborough, including part of the Road of Dala (Slige Dala Meic Umhoir), an ancient trackway running south from the Hill of Tara. Shean's owner, Colonel Whitney, had become 'greatly indebted' to Daniel who proposed that if Whitney married his daughter, he would not only 'forgive the debt, but redeem his estate from all other incumbrances [sic]'. Whitney refused, declaring that he 'could not think of smothering his blood by marrying a tailor's daughter'. Daniel called in the debt. Realizing he would now have to sell his estate, Whitney advised Daniel that he had thought the matter through and maybe marrying a tailor's daughter wasn't such a bad idea after all. This time it was Daniel's turn to decline on the basis that he could not possibly allow his beloved daughter to marry a man on the cusp of selling up. Whitney folded and Daniel bought the Shean estate.

He permitted Whitney to remain in the castle at Shean, but the colonel continued to mock his professional status. On one occasion, he was invited to dinner at the castle. Whitney, who had ensured there was no knife or fork in front of his guest, invited him to tuck in. 'There is plenty of meat, but nothing to cut it,' said Daniel. 'Why don't you draw your scissors and clip it, Sir?' suggested Whitney. 'I drew it time enough to clip the lordship of Shean from your back, Sir,' retorted Tailor Byrne, for which he was ordered 'to quit the Castle'.

In 1664, Daniel secured confirmation of his right to a coat of arms based on that of the O'Byrnes of Glenmalure, County Wicklow, the principal dynasty from whom he claimed a direct lineal descent. Seven years later, he bought his eldest son Gregory the baronetcy of Timogue, to be held for him and his male heirs forever. However, Sir Gregory, who studied law at Gray's Inn in London, appears to have got somewhat ahead of himself. While walking with his old man through the streets of Dublin one day, he said: 'Father, you ought to walk to the left of me, I being a knight and you but a mechanic.' 'No, you puppy,' replied Daniel. 'I have the precedency in three ways: first, because I am an older man; secondly, because I am your father; and thirdly, because I am the son of a gentleman, and you are but the son of a poor taylor [sic].'

When he died in 1684, Daniel was buried as a Catholic in Dublin's St Audeon's Church alongside his wife Anne, mother of their seven children. She was the daughter of a Dublin merchant, Richard Taylor of Swords; the Taylor family name adds another layer to Daniel's earlier retort to his son's impudence.

Sir Gregory became a tax assessor for the Queen's County and served as a member in the Patriot Parliament called by the pro-Catholic king, James II. As a captain in the Royal Irish Regiment of Foot, he served for the King at both the Siege of Derry in 1688–89 and the Battle of the Boyne; his younger brother Joseph was killed in action at the Battle of Aughrim. Sir Gregory later appears to have gone into exile in France, dying in 1712. He was ancestor of both the Polish O'Byrne family (also known as d'Obyrn or Obyrn) and the von Obyrns of Saxony in Germany.

20 The Byerley Turk: A Warhorse on the Boyne

 It was still early morning on 1 July 1690 when Colonel Robert Byerley led his Turkish stallion into the waters of the Boyne, near Oldbridge in County Meath. His men followed close behind, some carrying sea-green standards that floated in the breeze. Each horse was decorated in ribbons, each cavalryman's hat adorned with green branches. A division of King William's infantry advanced alongside them, urged onwards by the Duke of Schomberg, William of Orange's trusted commander. At length the seventy-five-year-old duke ordered his troops to form a line. Colonel Byerley and the Queen Dowager's Horse unsheathed their glittering swords and pointed them forwards. And then, with a nod from Schomberg, they charged. The Battle of the Boyne was underway.

The battle marked one of the pivotal moments in the Williamite War of 1688–91, in which the mostly Catholic, Jacobite followers of James II, the deposed Stuart king of England,

Scotland and Ireland, took on the mostly Protestant supporters of William III, or William of Orange, the Dutch prince who had deposed him. It can be a complicated war to make sense of. Take, for instance, the two kings. William was James II's nephew, but James was also William's father-in-law. Or, try this: William's Protestant army was bankrolled by Pope Innocent XI, who lent him 150,000 *scudi*, the equivalent of about £3.5 million today. Leopold I, the staunchly Catholic Holy Roman Emperor, also backed William. In the other corner, James had the support of Louis XIV, the 'Sun King' of France, who sent six thousand French soldiers to support the Stuart cause.

The war is also notable for the dark brown warhorse that Colonel Byerley rode throughout the campaign. Every thoroughbred horse that races today in Britain or Ireland can trace its ancestry to one of three stallions – the Godolphin Barb, the Darley Arabian or, the earliest of these foundation sires, the Byerley Turk. The horse is believed to have been foaled in Serbia, then part of the Turkish or Ottoman Empire, in 1678. He had a bulkier frame than most Arabians and was distinctive for his large eyes, 'high carriage of the tail' and 'prominent knees'. Trained as a cavalry horse, he was 'schooled to the cannons' by the time he participated in the Battle of Vienna in 1683. The story runs that Byerley captured his handsome charger in the wake of the Turkish defeat at Buda three years later.

Robert Byerley was born in 1660, the fourth son of a decorated cavalry commander who had fought for the Royalists during the English Civil War. Robert's grandfather was killed in action during the same conflict. At the age of fourteen, Robert inherited his father's estate in Durham, England. A decade later, when James II succeeded to the throne, he was elected to Parliament for County Durham.

Although he opposed many of the new king's pro-Catholic policies, Byerley loyally helped the monarch defeat the Duke of Monmouth, an illegitimate son of the late Charles II who attempted to seize the crown. However, after Monmouth's execution, Byerley began to have grave misgivings about James II. Sidelined for refusing to accede to the King's increasingly dictatorial behaviour, he threw in his lot with William of Orange when the Dutch prince – the husband to James II's daughter Mary – invaded England and deposed James in what became known as the Glorious Revolution.

The ensuing conflict soon spilled into Ireland where James II found considerable support among a Catholic population still reeling from the Tudor and Cromwellian conquests. King William began sending forces to Ireland, including Lieutenant Colonel Byerley, who sailed for Belfast in the autumn of

1689, accompanied by his trusty charger. Horse and rider would serve together in Ireland for the next two years, during which time Byerley emerged as one of King William's most effective cavalry commanders.

Byerley was still in Ulster on 15 March 1690 when he found the perfect opportunity to exhibit his magnificent stallion. He entered him in a military race that took place at the Flying Horse Crossroads outside Downpatrick, the site of the original Down Royal racecourse. Byerley's Turk, as his horse was now known, duly triumphed over the 4.8-km (3-mile) horseshoe-shaped course and won the top prize, the Silver Bell.

Three months later, Byerley and his charger were presented to King William at Hillsborough in County Down. The monarch had landed at Carrickfergus in County Antrim three days earlier. Within a week, Byerley's regiment was marching south with

William's army, reaching the banks of the River Boyne at the end of June. The battle that followed was a veritable epic, not least with the opposing kings lining out their armies on either side of the ancient river.

Ambushed by Jacobite cavalry during a reconnaissance mission on the eve of the battle, Byerley was fortunate that his steed's agility enabled him to escape certain death, but several of his men and horses were killed by a Jacobite cannonade that evening. This is said to have been the same cannonade that nearly obliterated William; the King managed to swivel just in time so that the blast merely grazed his right shoulder blade.

On the morning of the battle, a Jacobite officer named John Stevens took a walk along the south bank of the Boyne to assess the state of the two armies. To his mounting disgust, he noted a huge number of his own men sprawled unconscious along the riverbank. The air reeked of brandy. In his journal, Captain Stevens would later explain how King James had 'appointed brandy to be distributed to each regiment' in order to cheer the men 'for the fatigue of the day'. However, there had been such a hold-up in the delivery of the brandy that when the barrels finally arrived, the soldiers had gone berserk, abandoning their orderly lines, ripping the lids off the barrels and thrusting their kettles into the alcohol-filled vats. As Stevens grimly noted, they 'drank so extravagantly that I am sure above 1000 men were thereby tendered unfit for service, & most were left dead drunk scattered about the fields'.

Even as Stevens was surveying the drunken Jacobites, King William's army was about to make its opening move. Byerley was with the cavalry when it crossed a ford in the river that morning and charged the Jacobite lines, spreading over the surrounding cornfields, galloping up laneways, leaping over ditches and tearing at the enemy with its swords. It was not a victory easily won but William's triumph at the Boyne was a massive step towards securing Protestant dominance in Britain and Ireland. Within days, James II had fled from Ireland while William's exultant forces mustered at Finglas in north Dublin.

Byerley was again presented to King William who thanked him for his good conduct. He then advanced south in pursuit of the Jacobite army, which was so badly stung by James II's lousy leadership at the Boyne that disgruntled Jacobite soldiers now referred to him as Séamus an Chaca, or 'James the Shit'. Byerley spent the following summer leading his regiment into action in Kilkenny, Waterford and Clonmel in County Tipperary, helping to capture each town in turn. They reached Limerick at the end of August but the Williamites were unable to crack the city, not least because a band of Jacobite guerrilla fighters, known as rapparees, destroyed their principal siege weapons.

Byerley was appointed governor of Mountmellick, a Williamite stronghold in the Queen's County, from where he conducted a brutal campaign to hunt down rapparees. At his command were fifty sabre-rattling horsemen and three hundred musket-wielding infantry who he led out on numerous deadly forays against the rebels in and around Portarlington, Rosenallis and Brittas. He also quashed a number of attempts to surprise and burn Mountmellick itself.

In the summer of 1691, the Byerley Turk served at both the Siege of Athlone and the Battle of Aughrim, where Byerley's cavalry once again galloped at full pelt into the enemy lines, slashing, hacking, cutting and firing. The Jacobites were completely overpowered, losing between five thousand and seven thousand dead. This battle – a bigger and bloodier event than the Boyne – marked the end for the Jacobites, who surrendered

Limerick that autumn. In November 1691, Byerley shipped his now-famous warhorse back to England and put him out to stud at Middridge Grange, his family seat in Durham. Byerley also retired from army life at this time, possibly due to an injury picked up in Ireland.

In 1692, he married his beautiful cousin, Mary Wharton, the wealthy heiress to the Goldsborough estate in North Yorkshire. She descended from Henry VIII's illegitimate son by Mary Boleyn, who was the Tudor king's mistress just before he so fatefully turned his eyes on her younger sister Anne. The Whartons also owned substantial lands in Ireland, primarily in counties Westmeath and Carlow. One of Mary's cousins was credited with composing 'Lilli Burlero', the marching jig of the Williamite army, which ridiculed James and his Jacobite supporters.

The newlyweds moved to Goldsborough Hall, where they raised two sons and three daughters while Byerley focused on 'agricultural pursuits'. A leading High Church Tory, he represented Knaresborough in nine parliaments before his death aged seventy-one in 1731. The Byerley Turk proved 'a most excellent stallion' and the British aristocracy was soon queuing up for his offspring; his progeny would become prized possessions of the racing elite all across Europe. The venerable warhorse died at Goldsborough in 1706 and was buried on the estate. His descendants include Anthony Van Dyck (winner of the 2019 Epsom Derby), Masar (winner of the 2018 Epsom Derby), Frankel (the highest-rated racehorse in the world in 2011 and 2012) and Galileo (winner of the 2001 Epsom Derby, and the leading sire in Great Britain and Ireland in 2008 and, consecutively, from 2010 through 2018).

21 The Lixnaw Project

One of the most remarkable landscaping projects of the 17th century took place along the banks of the River Brick at Lixnaw, some 11 km (6½ miles) southwest of Listowel, in the plains of north County Kerry. This was the demesne of William FitzMaurice, 20th Lord of Kerry, who lived at Lixnaw Court, a five-bay, two-storey Jacobean mansion that he built in 1680. It stood opposite a castle where his ancestors had lived for the previous four hundred years. Nicholas, the 3rd Lord, erected a stone bridge across the river in 1320 and so became 'the first person that made causeways to this place, the land being naturally wet and marshy'.

During the 1680s and 1690s, Lord Kerry's employees completely changed the surrounding terrain. They constructed a new road along a man-made dyke that ran across the marsh, bookended by a mausoleum and an oblong tower, known as the Hermitage, visible from the main house. They built a series of walled courts, gardens, orchards and summerhouses, as well as an octagonal house that may have been used for cock-fighting. They also cut three shapely canals into the meandering, tidal Brick and created a bathing pool in the gardens where the FitzMaurices' guests could splash about. The canals were particularly impressive as they not only provided an aesthetic vista but also helped to drain the surrounding farmlands. The hardworking steward who oversaw this remarkable operation was Connemara-born Seán Mór Seoighe (Big John Joyce), a direct ancestor of the writer James Joyce and of the historian and music collector Patrick Weston Joyce.

One early admirer of Joyce's work was Dr Charles Smith, the Irish topographer, who observed in 1750 how the tidal canals flowed right into Lixnaw's gardens, such that 'boats of a considerable burden may bring up goods to the bridge near the house'.

Ninety years later, Samuel Lewis, another topographer, described how 'sea-weed and sand for manure' were still being brought up the river to the village of Lixnaw, which, at that time, comprised 'two streets of tolerably good houses', as well as a 'spacious' Catholic chapel and a school. Mr Lewis also mentioned an unfulfilled ambition by the Scottish engineer Alexander Nimmo to make the river navigable for larger vessels and to drain and cultivate extensive tracts of marsh and bogland nearby.

When William FitzMaurice died in 1697, he was succeeded by his son Thomas who became the Earl of Kerry in 1723. His wife Anne was a daughter of Sir William Petty, the scientist, philosopher and political economist who surveyed Ireland for Oliver Cromwell in the 1650s. Jonathan Swift described Anne as 'egregiously ugly, but perfectly well bred'. She was also wealthy enough to add two wings to her husband's castellated mansion,

as well as a fine library and a private chapel, lined with copies of the prestigious Raphael Cartoons from Hampton Court Palace.

Anne's grandson, the 3rd Earl of Kerry, had little love for Lixnaw and lived between France and England. By 1783, he had sold all of his Kerry estates to the Cork merchant Richard Hare, father of the 1st Earl of Listowel. The only property that the childless Lord Kerry retained was the mausoleum at Lixnaw where some of his forebears lay buried.

Among those who grew up at Lixnaw was William Petty, 2nd Earl of Shelburne, who had the misfortune to serve as prime minister (1782–83) during the final months of Britain's disastrous campaign in the American War of Independence. In 1839, his son, Henry, 3rd Marquess of Lansdowne (who also succeeded as 4th Earl of Kerry), was the Lord President of the Council who persuaded the House of Lords in London to spend about half a million pounds improving navigation along the River Shannon. Lansdowne Road and Shelbourne [sic] Road in Dublin are both named for the family.

Another child of Lixnaw was Lady Arabella Fitzmaurice Denny, the philanthropist who founded the Magdalen Asylum for Protestant Girls in Dublin in 1765. Horrified at the prospect of being buried alive, her will of 1792 directed that she be 'put in a leaden coffin, and my jugular veins opened, and then enclosed in an oak coffin and conveyed to the Church of Tralee'. The *Kerry Magazine* noted that the funeral of Lady Arabella, 'one of the most amiable women in Ireland', was attended by 'a large assemblage of all classes.... The most remarkable circumstance attending the funeral was the wailing of the twelve mourners.' These were twelve Kerry widows who had each received an annual gift of 'two suits of black' and 'donations at festivals' from Lady Arabella ever since the death of her husband, Colonel Denny.

The end was already nigh for Lixnaw by the time Arthur Young visited in 1773. Two hundred and fifty years later, Young's lament that 'all is desolation and everything in ruins' still accurately describes the scene. Thick banks of ivy now shroud the rough rubble ruins wherein the FitzMaurices slept and dined; the canals lie abandoned; the gardens are long gone and the carefully drained fields where Lord Kerry's cattle once grazed have been reclaimed by the voracious marshes.

22 Joshua Dawson, Spymaster

It is not generally acknowledged that Joshua Dawson – the builder of Dublin's Mansion House on Dawson Street – was once Ireland's foremost persecutor of Catholic priests. And yet that he was.

Born in 1660, Dawson was the scion of a Protestant family from England's Lake District who settled in County Derry; his grandfather purchased an estate (later Castle Dawson) near the north shore of Lough Neagh. By the time James II came to the throne in 1685, young Joshua was a civil servant at Dublin Castle, the principal seat of British authority in Ireland. He watched aghast as the openly Catholic monarch dismantled the Protestant state and began re-establishing both Britain and Ireland as Catholic dominions.

In 1691, William of Orange's army destroyed James II's forces (see chapter 20), paving the way for the infamous Penal Code, a series of laws that severely restricted the rights of Ireland's Catholic majority. They were prohibited from buying land

or carrying arms. Their churches were to have neither steeples nor crosses. Priests were forbidden from wearing clerical garb or holy emblems in public. No child was to be educated as a Catholic.

Meanwhile, Dawson rose through the ranks to become undersecretary to the Chief Secretary for Irish Affairs. In 1702 he was given the freedom of the City of Dublin. The following year, he established the Paper Office, a state bureau dedicated to duplicating every letter, order, petition and warrant that passed through Dublin Castle. Such zealous efficiency – and the vital information that came with it – propelled him to high office as Secretary to the Lords Justices by 1705; he effectively ruled Ireland for the next nine years.

As well as orchestrating troop movements, much of Dawson's time was spent monitoring the threat of invasion from French or Spanish privateers in support of the exiled James II or, after James's death in 1701, his son, 'James III' (aka the Pretender). Dawson's most dramatic role was to oversee a major clampdown on Catholic priests in Ireland. This intensified from 1701 when many priests opted to go on the run rather than comply with a new law insisting they swear an oath denouncing the Pretender's claims and affirming the Protestant right to the Crown. Determined to track down every renegade priest, Dawson established an intricate web of spies and informers in every major port and town in Ireland.

In 1709, a new law decreed that Ireland's 1,089 registered Catholic priests must swear an Oath of Abjuration by which they recognized the Protestant Queen Anne as Supreme Head of the Church of England and Ireland. When just 33 priests complied, Secretary Dawson swept down on the Catholic hierarchy. Such priests may have expected to be hanged for treason on Dawson's watch but, in fact, most were simply transported away from Irish shores and warned never to return.

As part of the process, Dawson began recruiting priest hunters. None were more effective than Edward Tyrrell, a money-lusting Catholic ex-con from Galway, who Dawson ingeniously placed as a spy at the Irish College at Leuven in Flanders. Tyrrell's reports were replete with the names of Irish families who had sent their children to be educated at Leuven or whose sons were now serving in the Catholic armies of Spain or France. As well as naming scores of priests in Ireland alleged to be Jacobite sympathizers, Tyrrell also kept Dawson up to speed about prominent Jacobite supporters like the 2nd Duke of Ormonde and Sir Henry Bunbury, Commissioner of the Revenue for Ireland.

In 1712, Tyrrell himself was arrested on a charge of bigamy, then considered an offence against God, punishable by death. At his trial in Dublin, he swore that he worked for Dawson but the Secretary denied him. Tyrrell was hanged on Gallows Hill near Baggot Street.

Dawson had been amassing property in the Irish capital for many years, including two pubs near the castle and 'a piece of marshy land without even a bare lane crossing it' that he drained and grandly called 'Dawson Street'. Within a decade, it was considered the finest street in Dublin and included the two-storey, red-brick Mansion House built for Dawson, now the city's oldest free-standing house. In 1714 Dawson sold the house to Dublin Corporation for £3,500 plus a yearly rent of 40 shillings and a 2.7-kg (6-lb) loaf of sugar every Christmas. It has been the Lord Mayor of Dublin's official residence since 1715.

Dawson died aged sixty-five in 1725, three years before the enactment of the final Penal Law by which all Catholics were deprived of the vote.

23 Lord Rosse & the Hell-Fire Club

Born in 1696, Richard Parsons, 1st Earl of Rosse, was one of the most colourful characters of the Georgian Age. He inherited his good looks from his mother, Elizabeth de Hamilton, the eldest of three beautiful French sisters. At the age of seventeen, he went to Oxford where he earned a reputation as an outstanding wit and an impressive drinker. Five years later, George I elevated him in the peerage as the Earl of Rosse. He married two heiresses in succession, each of whom bore him a son.

In June 1725, this 'consummate profligate' and well-known libertine was elected first Grand Master of the Grand Lodge of Ireland. His election continues to baffle Freemasons to this day because Freemasonry is all about moderation and obedience while Rosse was a champion of excess and debauchery. Dr Crawley, the eminent Masonic historian, conceded that 'His Lordship's idea of morals were inverted, and his skill shone most in the management of the small-sword and the dice-box.'

However, Lord Rosse was clearly as adept as he was persuasive; he was re-elected Grand Master in 1730.

The following year, Rosse inherited a million pounds from his immensely wealthy grandmother, Fanny Talbot, and stepped down as Grand Master. He then set off on an extended tour of Europe and Egypt, during which time he established himself as a 'sorcerer and dabbler in black magic'. He wrote a book called *Dionysus Rising*, which was purportedly based on an ancient scroll looted from the Great Library in Alexandria shortly before it burned to the ground. He is also reputed to have founded a society called the Sacred Sect of Dionysus, celebrating the joys of Bacchus and Venus, vis-à-vis alcohol and free love.

In about 1737, the Earl remerged on the Irish social scene, founding the notorious Hell-Fire Club, whose principal haunt was the Eagle Tavern on Cork Hill, near Dublin Castle. The 'Bucks', as they were known, sometimes met in Montpelier, an abandoned hunting lodge in the Dublin Mountains. Exactly what this secret society got up to remains a source of much gossip even today. The rumours alone would give Stephen King the shivers. Lord Rosse and his cronies are said to have hosted black masses, mock crucifixions and wild homosexual orgies, featuring women dressed as nuns. Black cats were reputedly sacrificed on the altar while the bucks drank hot *scaltheen*, a potent cocktail of whiskey and melted butter, and played cards with the Devil.

Satanism and an ill-informed black magic undoubtedly played a role in these gatherings – you'd expect as much from a club called Hell-Fire – but, in truth, this was little more than a bunch of young, thrill-seeking Protestant rakes who drank, gamed and wenched, albeit with a certain 18th-century panache. They were the sons of landed gentry, merchants and minor aristocracy with too much time on their hands and money to burn.

There was a dark side, however – the club's oath was vehemently anti-Catholic. One of its putative members, Richard 'Burn-Chapel' Whaley, was so called for his penchant for setting fire to the thatch on Catholic chapels, although the Protestant church was also targeted, with club members disrupting church services and streaking in front of bishops. Jonathan Swift, Dean of St Patrick's Cathedral at the time, declared them 'monsters'.

It was another member, Lord Santry, who brought the Hell-Fire Club crashing down. The alarm bells were triggered when he forced a sedan chairman to drink a bottle of brandy, then drenched him in spirits and set him alight, killing the poor man. When Santry subsequently ran his sword through an innocent tavern porter, he became the only member of the Irish House of Lords to be convicted of murder. He was sentenced to death but, after intensive lobbying by his friends, King George II reluctantly granted him a royal pardon.

Lord Rosse never lost his sense of humour. In 1741, as he lay dying at his townhouse on Dublin's Molesworth Street, he received a letter from Dean Madden of the nearby St Ann's Church, lambasting him as a blasphemer, scoundrel, gamester and such like, and imploring him to repent of his sins without delay. Noting that the Dean had simply addressed the letter to 'My Lord', Rosse put it into a fresh envelope and instructed a footman to deliver it to Lord Kildare who lived nearby. Kildare, one of Dean Madden's most pious and generous parishioners, was aghast to receive such a letter but Lord Rosse died before anybody worked it out. The Hell-Fire Club was disbanded following his death. In 1868, over one hundred years later, the present-day Freemasons' Hall was built on Molesworth Street, a stone's throw from his townhouse.

24 The Butcher's Column

In the heart of the Midlands town of Birr, County Offaly, stands an elaborate 13.5-m (44-ft)-high Doric pillar known as the Cumberland Column. Completed in 1747, it is the oldest such column in Ireland, constructed during a frenetic era of folly-building that also gave rise to the Boyne Obelisk (which was destroyed during the Irish Civil War), Connolly's Folly in County Kildare, and the Stillorgan Obelisk in Dublin.

The column in Birr celebrates the Duke of Cumberland, George II's favourite son, whose army crushed Bonnie Prince Charlie's Jacobite forces at the Battle of Culloden in 1746. It was arguably the House of Hanover's finest hour but Cumberland spoiled it all by allowing his victorious men to run riot through the Scottish Highlands on a barbaric killing spree, 'scorching the earth' so badly that Scotland was plunged into a dreadful famine. The American revolutionary Thomas Paine described it as 'one of the most shocking instances of cruelty ever practiced'.

The Scots would ever after recall Cumberland as the Butcher of Culloden but, while Bonnie Prince Charlie fled to France and drunken ignominy, the young duke was lionized as a British hero, the saviour of the Protestant faith. Parliament awarded him an annual income of £25,000, Trinity College Dublin elected him its chancellor and Handel dedicated an oratorio to him. Coins were minted, plates, bowls, mugs and punchbowls were produced in his honour, with mottoes such as 'Duke William For Ever', and he was toasted in taverns across the fledgling British Empire. His name graced streets and squares in London, Glasgow, Edinburgh and indeed, Birr.

In its glory days, the Cumberland Column in Birr was crowned by a 2.3-m (7.5-ft)-high white marble statue of 'The Butcher' himself, clad in the robes of a Roman senator; the column was modelled on that of Marcus Aurelius in Rome. On the day the statue was hoisted atop, the newly formed Birr Freemasons Lodge paraded gleefully around the town's equally new Palladian 'Cumberland Square' (now Emmet Square) before its members were treated to 'a most liberal entertainment' at Birr Castle where 'the same mirth was continued and toasts repeated'.

The central figure in all this was Sir Laurence Parsons, a prominent Freemason, who lived in the castle. His commissioning of the column was just the first phase of an ambitious but sadly unfulfilled plan to convert Birr into an extraordinary Gothic playground replete with fantastical fountains, grotesque grottoes and labyrinthine corridors modelled on Hell itself. The plans survive in an album entitled *Miscelanea Structura Curiosa*, which contains a series of architectural drawings attributed to Sir Laurence and his young cousin, the architect Samuel Chearnley. Both men were clearly influenced by the occult but the project fell apart with Chearnley's tragic and untimely death from illness shortly before the statue of Cumberland was raised

While the Cumberland Column stands yet, the statue of the Butcher has long vanished from its pedestal. Local legend holds that it was toppled by vengeful Scottish soldiers stationed nearby. The truth is rather less dramatic: the Urban District Council ordered its removal in 1915 when a crack caused it to tilt dangerously over the square below.

Whether Cumberland himself ever visited Birr is unknown. Like a football manager, a general is only as good as his last victory and he swiftly fell from grace when his army suffered back-to-back defeats against the French. Retiring from public life, the 'grossly corpulent' duke became known for his 'dull gallantries' with the prostitutes who frequented Marylebone Gardens in London. He died of a heart attack aged forty-four in 1765.

25 Peg Plunkett, Queen of Vice

Christmas 1794 was a distinctly uncomfortable time for a large number of the well-to-do men who frequented Georgian Dublin. The word was out that Mrs Leeson, long regarded as the city's foremost courtesan and brothel queen, was preparing her memoirs for publication. Her past conquests included a former viceroy, innumerable peers, a large number of the city's judicial, political and mercantile elite and several senior army officers and eminent clergymen. Panic swelled at the prospect of being named and shamed.

Margaret 'Peg' Plunkett, aka Mrs Leeson, was born in about 1742 and grew up in County Westmeath, where her Catholic parents had a whopping twenty-two children, of whom only eight survived to adulthood. When Peg's mother succumbed to fever, her inept father handed the property over to her brother Christopher, a bully with a 'tyrannic temper', who horsewhipped his sisters and prohibited them from marrying lest he have to cough up for a dowry. Peg eloped with a 'most engaging' young man but the runaways were caught; Christopher beat her so badly that she was confined to bed for three months.

At last she escaped to live with a sister in Dublin, where Mr Dardis, a family friend, 'snatch'd the glorious, golden opportunity' of her virginity, 'yet how could I call him seducer, when I met the seduction half way?' The romance resulted in a daughter but Peg was disowned by her family shortly before Dardis vanished. On 'the verge of perishing', as she put it, she resorted to her womanly charms. Her first lover was Abbey Street wine merchant Thomas Caulfield, who 'slipped two guineas into my bosom' and arranged for her to move to quarters 'more convenient' to his own. A son was born shortly before Caulfield also abandoned her.

And then came Joseph Leeson, son and heir of the 1st Earl of Milltown. Occasionally she journeyed with him to Russborough House, the stately County Wicklow mansion that his father had built in the 1740s. He also set her up with an apartment on Ranelagh Road but he grew increasingly possessive. Their relationship collapsed when a spy hired by Leeson reported that the moment he left the house, Peg opened the doors to let other lovers in. She was hurled out by Leeson, but adopted his surname nonetheless.

She spent the next three years living with a Mr Lawless, with whom she had five children. However, they gradually tired of each other's incessant affairs; the loss of all five children, one by one, must have been an insurmountable tragedy. Astonishingly, not one of the nine children Peg eventually bore survived childhood.

By 1763, Peg was on course to become the foremost courtesan in Dublin, sleeping with very rich men who fed, clothed, housed and entertained her in return. During the mid 1770s she

opened a brothel on Drogheda Street, hand-picking the most alluring beauties she could find. This prospered until 1779 when their plush quarters were destroyed by the Pinkindindies, a violent student gang from Trinity College named for their loathsome habit of 'pinking' or pricking innocent passers-by with their swords. Their leader Richard Crosbie would find fame in 1785 as the first Irishman to perform a manned ascent in a balloon. During the 1770s the gang went on the rampage through Dublin, raping women, vandalizing theatres, toppling lamp posts and raiding gambling dens. Peg, who miscarried on account of the attack, slammed her assailants: 'however they might be deemed gentlemen at their birth, or connexions, yet, by their actions, deserved no other appellation than that of RUFFIANS'.

After a short stint in London, Peg returned to Dublin and set up a new brothel near St Patrick's Cathedral. Complete with a fine garden, this became *the* place to go during this golden age of duelling and masquerades. As Peg put it, she was 'at the very zenith of my glory, the reigning vice queen of the Paphian Goddess'. She ensured her 'girls' were always splendidly turned out with diamonds, dresses, servants and carriages. Peg herself caused a sensation when she became the first woman in Dublin to sport a bell-hoop; ladies of society quickly followed her lead. Much of her success was based on appearance. Hence, while she did not particularly like champagne, she still asked for it whenever clients offered her a drink. For their part, she ensured her clients were fed upon fresh oysters and steamed asparagus, wellknown aphrodisiacs.

In 1784, she relocated to a finely furnished establishment at Pitt Street on the site of the present-day Westbury Hotel, where her most influential lover was the claret-loving viceroy, the Duke of Rutland. He was fated to die in Dublin in 1787, aged thirty-three, and is recalled by the Rutland Memorial Fountain on Merrion Square West.

The press followed her closely and admired her sense of humour; she attended a masquerade ball on College Green dressed as Artemis, goddess of chastity. She was on the quayside in 1788 to wave farewell to the notorious gambler and libertine Thomas 'Buck' Whaley when he set off to win a £15,000 bet by riding from Dublin to Jerusalem and back. She even showed up to watch her nemesis Crosbie take to the skies in his balloon.

Peg's personal fortune was briefly boosted when Viscount Yelverton paid her 500 guineas to stop seeing his feckless son. Her other clients included John Philpot Curran, the pro-Catholic orator and lawyer, and David La Touche, the Governor of the Bank of Ireland, although she ejected the Earl of Westmorland, the 'despicable' viceroy, for treating his wife so disgracefully.

In 1792, Peg sold up, moved to Blackrock and announced her intention of living 'a sober and godly life'. On the basis that gentlemen always pay their debts, her intention was to simply cash in on the large number of IOUs and promissory notes she had racked up during the preceding decades. For such a worldly woman, her retirement plan was astoundingly naive. Her debtors, or most of them, failed to pay. As she had left the game, her payment requests were not taken seriously.

Peg still had some cards to play, namely her memoirs. As well as bringing in badly needed cash, the very prospect of Dublin's best-known courtesan and brothel-keeper going public with her story would surely make some of her debtors come clean. The first two volumes were published in 1795, earning Peg £500, with a suitably provocative title: *Memoirs of Mrs. Margaret Leeson, Written by Herself, and Interspersed with Several Interesting and Amusing Anecdotes, of Some of the Most Striking Characters of Great*

Britain and Ireland. The books were snapped up by women eager to see if 'Mrs Leeson' had named either their own menfolk or the seemingly upstanding gentlemen who were courting them or their spinster daughters. In fact, both volumes were relatively tame. As Peg put it, those looking for 'some nice tit bits, and delicious morsels of scandal' would be disappointed, but she did include an unveiled threat: 'I shall in my next volumes, lay before the public a list of all who are in debt to me, with the sum, and how long owing.'

Peg's memoirs sold well but the money did not come in quickly enough. To her horror, she was arrested by bailiffs and lodged in a 'sponging house' (a private debtors' prison) where she remained until a friend raised funds to clear her debts. The incarceration took its toll; she grew so wan that friends could barely recognize her. Somehow, she managed to complete the third volume of her memoirs but, with an almost non-existent income, her morale was at a complete low when she and a friend were attacked and raped by a gang in Drumcondra over Christmas 1796. Both women contracted venereal disease, which developed into a fatal fever for Peg. She died at Fownes Street on 22 March 1797 and was buried at St James's Church graveyard, next to the Guinness Brewery.

Published posthumously, the third volume was much the juiciest and named many past clients such as Waddell Cunningham, a Belfast shipping tycoon and slave-trader, who she brilliantly described as 'that ungrateful old letcher, who while his amiable wife lay barren by his side, for forty-five years and more, made a shift to knock triplets out of his kitchen maid'. With details such as this, many of her clients not yet named must have breathed a huge sigh of relief when it emerged that the late Mrs Leeson had planned a fourth volume.

26 The Cherokee Club

 In 1792 the *Astrologer's Magazine & Philosophical Miscellany* warned readers of a new scourge in the Irish capital: 'A club called the CHEROKEES has been instituted in Dublin, by a set of uncivilised barbarians, of family and fortune. They have been lately dispersed, by the activity of the Magistracy, but not before two of the RUFFIANS were sent to Newgate, for attempting to tomahawk a lady of fashion in a sedan chair.'

The Cherokee Club was reputedly formed by 'the most dashing and care-driving members of Daly's and the Kildare Street clubs' in Dublin and owed its name to Joseph Leeson, 2nd Earl of Milltown, the former lover of Peg Plunkett (see previous chapter), who once described guests at a party he hosted at Russborough House as being 'as clamorous as Cherokees'. The mostly aristocratic members were free-thinking, beautifully dressed young bucks who relished in womanizing, drinking, gambling and, above all, disrupting public entertainments.

A satirical exposé published in the *Hibernian Magazine* claimed that aspiring members had to satisfy ten conditions before they could join the club. The first was that 'a candidate should have carried off and debauched a maid, a wife and a widow, or an indefinite number of each'. They were to be highly skilled fencers and marksmen and to have fought at least three duels, while to become club president, it was 'absolutely requisite' to have 'killed at least one man in a duel, or a waiter in a violent passion'.

The exposé also claimed that each Cherokee had to be able to drink six bottles of claret and a bumper (brim-filled glass) of cherry brandy at a single sitting. It was elsewhere stated that any Cherokee found sober after dinner was subject to a fine of £30 for a first offence, £50 for a second and expulsion from the club for a third. While the *Hibernian* article intended to lampoon the club, its purported rules were destined to become part of Cherokee folklore, supported by the sighting of a convoy of thirty 'cars', loaded with fine wines, leaving Dublin for the country residence of one member.

Having drunk themselves into a raucous stupor, the Cherokees then advanced onto the streets of Dublin to cause mayhem. Their assaults began with cat-calls, 'war-hoops' and whistling, but became increasingly violent. Their favourite target was the Lying-in (or Rotunda) Hospital on Rutland Square (now Parnell Square), the public rooms of which were regarded as the city's most fashionable entertainment venue, hosting a non-stop medley of concerts, masquerades and promenades. Such was the belligerence of the Cherokee attacks that the Rotunda was temporarily closed. They also broadened their quarry, randomly molesting lone men and women on the streets. By the autumn of 1792, few Dublin citizens dared go out after dark unarmed.

Despite widespread condemnation, no Cherokees were brought to trial, largely because of their family connections. As well as at least six MPs, the club included the future marquesses of Conyngham and Ormonde and, briefly, Buck Whaley. By the close of 1792, the outcry against the Cherokees in both the Dublin press and judicial quarters had reached a crescendo and there was a heavy and successful clampdown. While there were still no arrests, the Cherokees' immoral lifestyle often came at a cost to their personal health and wealth; many were said to be broken men by the age of thirty.

27 Gold Fever in Avoca

Avoca, County Wicklow, was the setting for an extraordinary gold rush in the latter months of 1795. Most present-day accounts state that the 'rush' began when a large nugget of 'pure virgin gold' was found in the Ballin valley stream by workers felling trees on Lord Carysfort's estate near Avoca. Another story suggests that a schoolteacher spotted the gold while walking along the banks of the appropriately named Goldmines River.

Neither proposition, however, tallies with that of *Saunders's News-Letter* of 13 October 1795, which outlined how the Avoca Gold Rush had started with a family feud the previous month. The Rosels, who farmed the area, had been quietly locating and selling gold for over a decade until a particularly large find prompted a row between two Rosel cousins. When one cousin beat up the other, the latter spilled the beans, 'and thus set thousands of the neighbourhood on the search, in consequence of which many thousand ounces of gold have been found within the last few weeks'. The newspaper added that 'above 4,000 people' had been out prospecting the previous Sunday. Within six weeks, more than £11,000-worth of gold was panned.

The Avoca Mines had been dubbed 'Little Peru' by the time the government took over management of them, appointing three directors under an act of Parliament. The works were destroyed during the 1798 Rebellion when the United Irishmen, a republican organization, launched an abortive insurrection to overthrow the government. The mine's directors subsequently applied for government funding to hack into the surrounding mountains 'in search of auriferous veins'. Nothing of value emerged from the drilling and, with the stream itself already so exhaustively panned, the works were abandoned and the gold rush petered out.

Nonetheless, by 1830 an estimated 217.7–280 kg (7,000–9,000 oz t) of gold had been extracted from the alluvial gravels of the Goldmines River. A 682-g (22-oz t) Avoca gold nugget remains the biggest yet found in Britain or Ireland. It was apparently melted down to make a snuffbox for King George III. Casts of the nugget are now held by the National Museum of Ireland, the Geological Survey of Ireland and the Natural History Museum in London.

All this was enough to inspire the Irish political heavyweight Charles Stewart Parnell to launch numerous prospecting operations in the area in the latter half of the 19th century. Parnell, who lived at nearby Avondale, loved nothing more than assaying small pieces of quartz found in local streams. His widow later recalled how he spent five years working on various chunks 'till he had extracted sufficient gold to line my wedding ring, even though his hope of getting enough for the whole ring was not fulfilled'.

They say that Avoca has long since been all played out but I went panning in the Goldmines River with some pals a couple of decades ago and we found enough gold to make a pair of earrings...for a butterfly. A tiny wisp of a flake but nonetheless it was gold. And that was enough to allow us to dream big as we slept in our riverside tents on that star-spangled night.

28 Medicinal Springs

In 1645, Gerard Boate, a Dutch physician, compiled a book called *Ireland's Naturall History* in which he homed in on Ireland's spas, writing: 'A few yeares since some Fountains have been discovered in Ireland, some of them not far from Dublin, and others in other parts, whose veines running through certain Minerals, and washing off the vertue of the same, yeeld a Medicinall water, apt to open the obstructions of man's body, and to cure other accidents thereof; which kind of Fountains are commonly called Spaes.'

The spa near Dublin to which Dr Boate referred was probably the one at Lucan, where its chalybeate springs had long been admired for the high content of iron salts. In about 1758, the sulphurous activity of the mineral springs that bubbled alongside this stretch of the River Liffey whipped up the nostrils of the local landowner, the splendidly named Agmondesham Vesey, who swiftly espied its commercial value. He enclosed the spring in a wall (thus protecting it against any potential deluges from the river) and opened it up as a healing well. He also sold bottles of 'Lucan Water' to the citizens of Dublin, through the Hammond Lane drug-shop of apothecary James McDonald, promising that each bottle was 'taken up in the proper Season, corked and carefully waxed'.

By 1760, John Hill, a well-known quack, was specifically recommending Lucan Water as a remedy for the kidney pain known as 'Gravel and Stone'. A decade later, John Rutty, a Dublin-born Quaker physician, was likewise promoting Lucan Water as a cure for skin diseases such as leprosy, eczema and general 'eruptions', as well as rheumatism, tuberculosis, gout, impetigo, herpes and dyspepsia. Dr Rutty observed of the spa itself: 'It may be smelt at the distance of many yards, especially in frosty, or in rainy weather. It is limpid, and in the well has a bluish cast, and throws up a white bluish scum to the surface.... [The water has] the flavour of a boiled egg, and when strongest, of a semi-putrid egg.'

In 1786, the topographer William Wilson listed sixteen spas in his *Post-Chaise Companion* for Irish travellers, the *Lonely Planet* of its day. Of Lucan, he wrote: 'by the river side is a noted medicinal spring, the waters of which are of great efficacy in many disorders. The well is sheltered in a deep niche, neatly executed in hewn stone. There is a rural thatched seat for the water drinkers and space allowed for walking about.'

The Lucan Spa was only 13 km (8 miles) west of Dublin City, a relatively safe and peaceful journey in the Georgian Age, and it consequently became the most popular spa in Ireland. As the *Dublin Evening Post* recorded in the summer of 1790, those who came 'seem well disposed to contribute to each other's amusement: and as the waters of its salubrious Spa are drunk nowhere in such perfection as at the fountain head, health adds its inducements to pleasure'.

By 1792, a crescent of thirty terraced houses had been constructed at Lucan for longer-term visitors. That year Mr Kearns, 'proprietor of the Well', converted a building above the spa into a 'most commodious' hotel for 'Ladies and Gentlemen', offering 'a variety of wines of the best quality'. By 1795, the hotel included a ballroom, a coach house for carriages and ample stabling for horses, along with 'plenty of the best hay and oats: his grass fields are in view of the lodger's windows'. The hotel began hosting regular concerts, balls and public breakfasts; circuses and carnivals also began to abound.

The 'fashionable' crowds making their way through the Liffey Valley were soon rivalling the numbers who flocked to the great English spas of Tunbridge Wells, Buxton and Leamington. Every Sunday, the road to Lucan was crammed with thousands

of Dubliners coming on foot, horseback, jaunting car and coach to enjoy the ambience and drink the water directly at the Spa House, a small hut built over the actual spring. For those who could not get to the spa, bottles of Lucan Water were exclusively on sale in Dublin either from Mr Thwaite's of 23 Lower Ormond-quay or Mr Herbert's of Great Britain Street.

In 1797, the hotel was taken over by Thomas Canavan. He had previously run a 'perfectly well-aired' boarding house in Lucan, at which prospective guests were charily advised: 'No Lady or Gentleman will be received until it is known particularly who they are.' However, the outbreak of the United Irishmen's ill-fated rebellion in the summer of 1798 inevitably saw business plunge for the fastidious Mr Canavan. He placed an advertisement early in the new year, promising that 'tranquillity is restored

in the neighbourhood, and a Captain's guard is stationed on the Crescent'. As a further inducement, he added that the hotel was 'supplied with goat's whey'.

Mr Canavan's fate is unknown but, in 1807, the hotel was taken up by John Collins, a former butler to the banking tycoon David La Touche. Mr Collins used his extensive experience of travelling 'both at home and on the Continent' to revamp the property in a style 'of appropriate elegance'. He was still in charge in 1831 when the officers of the 12th Lancers hosted a ball for four hundred people, headed up by the Duke and Duchess of Leinster.

The popularity of the Lucan Spa waned with the advent of sea-bathing and the coming of the Railway Age. By 1846, the hotel had become a school for clergymen. It was later used by the eye-catchingly named Institution for Imbeciles and Middle-Class Lunatics of Lucan as an asylum for the children of such unfortunates.

In 1891, a group of businessmen reignited interest in the spa by constructing the one-hundred-room Lucan Hydropathic and Spa Hotel on a hill behind the original hotel. An entire wing was devoted to treatments, with pumps connected directly to the springs, as well as an underground tunnel. The hotel was conveniently located along the Midland Great Western Railway line from Galway to Dublin. The Dublin and Lucan Steam Tramway also brought customers directly from the Irish capital to 'take the waters'; in return, the water was transported in bulk to Dr Steven's Hospital in Dublin. Mr Kearns's original Spa Hotel survives today as the County Bar, while there are still some vestiges remaining of the wall that Mr Vesey built to prevent his well from flooding over 260 years ago.

29 The Night of the Big Wind

The Night of the Big Wind was the most devastating storm in recorded Irish history. The hurricane of 6–7 January 1839 made more people homeless in a single night than all the sorry decades of eviction that followed it.

The calm before the Big Wind struck was particularly eerie. Most of the eight million people living in Ireland at the time were preparing for Little Christmas, the Feast of the Epiphany. The previous day had seen the first snowfall of the year, heavy enough for some to build snowmen. By contrast, Sunday morning was unusually warm, almost clammy, and yet the air was so still that, along the west coast, voices could be heard floating on the air between houses more than 1.6 km (1 mile) apart.

At approximately 3 p.m. on the 6th, the rain began to fall and the wind picked up. Nobody could have predicted that those first soft raindrops signified an advance assault from the most terrifying hurricane in human memory. By 6 p.m., the winds had become strong and the raindrops were heavier, sleet-like, with occasional bursts of hail. Farmers grimaced as their hayricks and thatched roofs took a pounding. In the towns and villages, fires flickered and doors slammed, church bells chimed and dogs began to whine. Fishermen turned their ears west; a distant, increasingly loud rumble could be heard upon the frothy horizon.

At Glenosheen in County Limerick, a well-to-do German farmer called Jacob Stuffle began to pray. At Moydrum Castle in County Westmeath, seventy-eight-year-old Lord Castlemaine decided an early bed was in order. In the Wicklow Mountains, a team of geographic surveyors headed up by John O'Donovan finally made it to their hotel in Glendalough; they had been walking all day, often knee-deep in snow. Sailing upon the Irish Sea, Captain Smyth of the *Pennsylvania* studied his instruments and tried to make sense of the fluctuating pressures.

By 10 p.m., Ireland was in the throes of a ferocious cyclone that would continue unabated through the night for at least eight hours. The hurricane had roared across 4,800 km (3,000 miles) of unbroken, island-free Atlantic Ocean, gathering momentum every second. It hit Ireland's west coast with such power that the waves are said to have broken over the top of the Cliffs of Moher in County Clare. Reading contemporary accounts, the impression is that if Ireland did not have such magnificent cliffs forming a barrier along its west coast, the entire country would simply have been engulfed by water. The noise of the sea crashing against the rocks could be heard for miles inland, above the roar and din of the storm itself. The earth trembled under the assault; the ocean tossed huge boulders onto the clifftops of the Aran Islands.

Perhaps the most distressing aspect was that all this took place in utter darkness. People cannot have known what was

going on. The wind churned its way across the land, extinguishing every candle and lantern it encountered. The black night was only relieved by the lightning streaks that accompanied the storm and the occasional blood-red flicker of the aurora borealis burning in the northern sky.

All across Ireland, hundreds of thousands of people awoke to the sound of the furious tempest, their windows shattered by hailstones, their brick walls rattling, their rain-sodden thatched roofs sinking fast. As the wind grew stronger, it began to rip the roofs off houses. Chimney pots, broken slates, sheets of lead and shards of glass were hurtled to the ground. Rather astonishingly, a statistic was later produced that 4,846 chimneys were knocked off their perches during the Night of the Big Wind.

Many of those who died that night were killed by falling masonry. Norman tower houses and old churches collapsed. Factories and barracks were destroyed. Fires erupted in the streets of Castlebar in County Mayo, Athlone in County Westmeath and Dublin. The wind blew all the water out of the canal at Tuam in County Galway. It knocked a pinnacle off Carlow Cathedral and the solitary remaining chimney off Carlow Castle. It stripped the earth alongside the River Boyne, exposing the bones of soldiers killed in the famous battle 150 years earlier.

Roads in every parish became impassable. All along the Grand Canal, trees were pulled up by the roots and hurled across the water to the opposite bank. Thousands of timber cabins were destroyed. Surviving inhabitants had no choice but to flee into the pitch-black night in clothes that were soon wholly drenched by the intense rains and snows that accompanied the cruel, piercing wind. Many sought shelter amid the hollows and hedges of the land.

Farmers were hit particularly hard. Hayricks in fields across Ireland were blown to pieces. Wooden fences and dry-stone walls collapsed, allowing terrified livestock to run away. Sheep were blown off mountains or killed by tumbling rocks. Cattle were reported to have simply frozen to death in the fields. The next morning, one of Jacob Stuffle's neighbours recalled seeing the distraught German standing high up on a hillock looking with dismay at his haggard farm, his stacks having been swept out of existence. Suddenly, he raised his two hands, palms open, high over his head, and looking up at the sky he roared in a voice that was heard far and wide, 'Oh, God Almighty, what did I ever do to You and You should treat me in that way!'

Stuffle was not the only man who believed that the hurricane, occurring on the night of the Epiphany, was of divine origin. Many saw it as a warning that the Day of Judgment would soon be upon them. Some believed the Freemasons had unleashed the Devil from the Gates of Hell. Others maintained that English fairies had invaded Ireland and forced the indigenous Little People to disappear amid a ferocious whirlwind. (Irish fairies, of course, are wingless and can only fly by calling up the *sidhe chora* – the magic whirlwinds.)

The well-to-do did not escape; many mansions had their roofs stripped off. Lord Castlemaine was fastening his bedroom windows when the storm blew them open and hurled him 'so violently upon his back that he instantly expired'. His brother-in-law, the Earl of Clancarty, later reported the loss of nearly 20,000 trees on his estate at Ballinasloe in County Galway. Similar figures came in from other landed estates; Henry Bruen of Oak Park in County Carlow declared that his woods were now 'as bald as the palm of my hand'. At the Seaforde estate in County Down, an estimated 60,000 trees were felled; the Marquess of Conyngham lost a third of his woods at Slane in County Meath. On 6 January 1839, timber was a valuable commodity. Twenty-four hours later, so many trees had fallen that it was virtually worthless. Unimagined numbers of wild birds were killed, their nesting places smashed and there was little birdsong that spring. Even crows and jackdaws seemed on the verge of extinction.

In his hotel room in Glendalough, John O'Donovan was fortunate not to share Lord Castlemaine's fate. He was struggling with the shutters when 'a squall mighty as a thunderbolt' propelled him across the room. When he viewed the damage next morning, he described it as if 'the entire country had been swept clean by some gigantic broom'.

Dublin resembled 'a sacked city...the whirlwind of desolation spared neither building, tree nor shrub'. The Liffey rose by several feet and overflowed the quay walls. The elms that graced the main thoroughfare of Phoenix Park were completely levelled, as were the elms at the Royal Hospital Kilmainham. The trees on Leinster Lawn outside the present-day Dáil Éireann (Irish Parliament) were uprooted and scattered 'like prostrate giants on their mother earth'.

The back wall of the Guinness Brewery collapsed, killing 'nine fine horses'. A witness next morning described how 'the noble animals [were] stretched everywhere as if sleeping, but with every bone crushed by the ponderous weight of the wall'. Military sentry boxes were blown off their stands and 'scattered like atoms'. A glass shop on Nassau Street became 'a heap of ruins'. On Clare Street, a chimney collapsed on a woman who had only just got into her bed, killing her instantly.

Police stations and churches opened their doors to thousands of frightened citizens who brought their young and frail in for protection. Even churches could not be trusted on this night of Lucifer. The steeple of Irishtown chapel caved in and the bell from the spire of St Patrick's Cathedral came down like a meteorite; mercifully nobody died in either instance. Phibsborough Road was a bombsite of exploded windows and fallen chimneys 'as if by shot and shell'.

One of the forty female inmates at the Bethesda Penitentiary on Dublin's north side took the opportunity to ignite a fire that destroyed the building as well as the surrounding houses, schoolhouse and chapel. Two firemen died trying to extinguish the flames.

The hurricane did not stop in Dublin. It pounded its way across the Irish Sea, killing hundreds of luckless souls caught at sea. It killed nearly one hundred fishermen off the east coast of Ireland by Skerries. It killed Captain Smyth and the thirty people on board the packet-ship *Pennsylvania*. Ships all along the west coast of England were wrecked; dead bodies continued to wash up onshore for weeks afterwards. At Everton, the same wind unroofed a cotton factory that whitened all the space for miles around, 'as if there had been a heavy fall of snow'.

Estimates as to how many died that night vary from three hundred to eight hundred, a remarkably low figure given the ferocity of the storm. Many more must have succumbed to pneumonia, frostbite or depression in its wake. Those bankrupted by the disaster included hundreds who had stashed their life savings up chimneys and in the thatched roofs that disappeared in the night.

Even in those days it was 'an ill wind that turned none to good' and among those to benefit were the builders, carpenters, slaters and thatchers who subsequently rebuilt the fallen buildings. The Big Wind also inspired the Rev. Romney Robinson of the Armagh Observatory to invent the Robinson Cupanemometer, which was to be the standard instrument for gauging wind speed for the rest of the 19th century.

Perhaps the most unlikely beneficiaries of the Night of the Big Wind were those old enough to remember it when the Old Age Pensions Act was enacted in January 1909, seventy years after the event. The Act, which offered the first-ever weekly pension to those over the age of seventy, was likened to the opening of a new factory on the outskirts of every town and village in Britain and Ireland.

By March 1909, over 80,000 'British' pensioners were registered, of whom 70,000 were Irish. Few births were registered in Ireland before civil registration began in 1864. As such, the Irish Pensions Committee decreed that if someone's age had 'gone astray' on them, they would be eligible for a pension if they could state that they were 'fine and hardy' on the Night of the Big Wind, or the Oíche na Gaoithe Móire, as it is called in Irish.

One such applicant was Tim Joyce of County Limerick. 'I always thought I was 60,' he explained. 'But my friends came to me and told me they were certain sure I was 70 and as there were three or four of them against me, the evidence was too strong for me. I put in for the pension and got it.'

30 The Crimean Banquet

Dublin, 1856. The city had never seen anything quite like it: over 3,600 bronzed and bearded redcoats marching eastwards along the quays on both sides of the River Liffey, pursued by carriages carrying their senior officers and other dignitaries. Some of the soldiers hobbled on crutches; others were missing arms or otherwise disfigured. Upon the breasts of their scarlet uniforms, each man sported the medal he had earned for his service in the British Army during its costly but ultimately victorious campaign against the dastardly Russians in the Crimean War.

Shortly after the long column passed the Custom House, the soldiers wheeled into a massive warehouse on the east side of George's Dock. The Tobacco Store (now known as the CHQ Building and home to EPIC – The Irish Emigration Museum) had been completely redesigned for the impending occasion – a massive banquet, paid for by the citizens of Dublin, to thank the veterans for their recent service.

In 1825, the government-owned warehouse and surrounding docks were leased to John and Harry Scovell, prominent wharf owners from Southwark in south London. Harry Scovell had been deputy assistant paymaster to the British Army during the Duke of Wellington's Iberian campaign in the Peninsular War (1808–14). His older brother Sir George Scovell was much revered for having cracked Napoleon's secret Grande Chiffre (Great Cipher) code, enabling the Iron Duke to oust the French from Andalusia in Spain and liberate Madrid.

At the conclusion of the Crimean War in February 1856, Harry Scovell was approached by Fergus Farrell, the Lord Mayor of Dublin. Mr Farrell, a former deputy to Daniel O'Connell, the Irish political giant, had long been haunted by the indifferent manner in which battle-scarred soldiers and sailors were treated after their return home from the Napoleonic Wars. As such, he conceived of the banquet as a way for Dubliners to show their appreciation to those who had just returned from the Crimea.

Ireland's role in the Crimean War is much understated. A number of the principal military leaders had Irish connections, including Lords Lucan, Gough and Raglan, as well as General Sir George de Lacy Evans, but it was at troop level that the Irish really made an impact. About a third of the 111,000 men who served were Irish. Many fought with regiments such as the 6th (Inniskilling) Dragoons (known as the Skins), the Connaught Rangers, the 8th King's Royal Irish Hussars, the 4th Royal Irish Dragoon Guards and the 18th (Royal Irish) Regiment of Foot. At least 114 of the cavalrymen who galloped into the Russian artillery guns during the Charge of the Light Brigade were Irish. The bugle that sounded that moment of glorious insanity was made in Capel Street, Dublin.

Some of the four thousand Irishmen serving in the Royal Navy were presumably cajoled into service by the moustachioed recruiting officer spotted strolling down Sir John Rogerson's Quay in Dublin back in 1854. Among them was Armagh-born Charles Lucas, a twenty-year-old mate on board HMS *Hecla* who heroically hurled a hissing Russian bomb off the ship's deck moments before it exploded. He duly became the first man to win a Victoria Cross and fetched up as a rear admiral. The first soldier to win a Victoria Cross was also an Irishman, namely Sergeant (later General Sir) Luke O'Connor from Elphin, County Roscommon. In total, thirty Irishmen won Victoria Crosses in the Crimean War.

Over one hundred Irishmen served as British Army surgeons, including Dr Philip Cross, later destined to swing for murdering his wife. Thirty-three Irish Sisters of Mercy and Sisters of Charity went out as nurses; some clashed with Florence Nightingale over how to treat the wounded. Eight Irish priests went as chaplains; three died.

All these connections evidently impressed Harry Scovell, who promptly offered the Tobacco Store to Lord Mayor Farrell free of charge. The engineer William Dargan, celebrated as 'the Father of Irish Railways', oversaw its conversion into a banqueting hall; he, too, refused a fee, and supplied the timber and other materials at his own expense. Walls were hung with the flags of Britannia and her Turkish, French and Sardinian allies. Muskets, swords and lances were fixed to the thirty-three iron pillars running through the building, while the iron roof trusses were painted red, white and blue. A bandstand was set up in the gallery, from which hung vast drapes bearing the names of the Crimean battles and major figures such as Lord Raglan and Miss Nightingale. Opposite the top table stood two huge burnished brass sculptures depicting a horse and gunner, made from Russian cannons that had been captured in the war.

Shortly before 11 a.m. on the unusually fine morning of 22 October 1856, a train arrived at Kingsbridge (now Heuston) Station carrying over a thousand soldiers from the Curragh Camp, Naas and Newbridge in County Kildare, and Carlow, Kilkenny and other military strongholds. They had been carried north *gratuit* by the Great Southern & Western Railway. Some fifteen hundred war veterans stationed in the various Dublin barracks joined them, along with another five hundred men from other provincial depots. As this combined force marched down the Liffey quays, the city was thronged with Dubliners waving their hats, cheering loudly and belting out rousing ballads. Among those marching was John Conolly of Celbridge, County Kildare, who had been awarded a Victoria Cross for repelling a Russian attack by wielding his brass telescope like a club during the Siege of Sebastopol.

At length the soldiers reached the Tobacco Store and in they marched, company by company, their medals gleaming on the same uniforms they had worn in the Crimea. Within thirty minutes, every man had taken his seat. There were 14 tables grouped around the upper hall, each laid out for 80 men, and a further 18 tables in the lower hall, each fitting between 122 and 148 men. In all, there were 3,628 soldiers seated, as well as the worthies on the top table, a special table for the band and a further 1,000 non-military guests, principally subscribers, seated in the gallery overlooking the hall. T & C Martin and Todd Burns supplied all the platforms, seating, tablecloths and other furnishings without a charge. 'When all were seated, and the sun shone in and lighted up in golden splendour the unparalleled scene, it was one of the grandest and most brilliant spectacles ever witnessed,' marvelled one participant.

Imagine the workload of the chefs of Messrs Spadaccini and Murphy as they set to work cooking this sumptuous feast in the kitchens of the Mansion House, Trinity College and Dublin Castle. The meat alone comprised 250 hams, 230 legs of mutton, 500 meat pies, 100 venison pasties, 200 turkeys, 200 geese, 250 pieces of beef, 100 capon cockerels and 6 ox-tongues. Everything was served cold except 3 tonnes of potatoes, boiled up at the North Union Workhouse, and 1.5 tonnes of plum pudding, cooked in the Lord Lieutenant's kitchen at Dublin Castle on the morning of the banquet and conveyed to the Tobacco Store by horse and cart. The wine merchant Henry Brennan donated a quart bottle of Dublin porter and a pint of choice port wine to each man.

At 1.30 p.m., Lord Mayor Farrell delivered grace and the men tucked in. The hum of conversation was so loud it must have sounded like an opera. What extraordinary dialogue surely passed between those heavily bearded and bushy-whiskered soldiers as they pondered the mayhem, triumphs and sorrows of that bungle-filled campaign between mouthfuls of succulent goose and plum pudding.

The party came to a swift end at 4.15 p.m. when the troops mustered in the Custom House yard and marched back to their respective trains. Whatever their thoughts of war and peace, there can be little doubt the soldiers got their rations' worth that day. The event was a huge public relations success, chronicled in detail in newspaper reports that were circulated far and wide across the British Empire.

There is a number of monuments to the Crimean War in Ireland today, including a stained-glass window in St Patrick's Cathedral, Dublin, and at least thirty captured Russian cannons and mortars scattered around the island. However, perhaps its most lasting legacy was the military camp at the Curragh of Kildare, which was established by the British Army in 1855 as a temporary training ground for ten thousand officers and soldiers bound for the Crimea. The camp proved such a success that it soon became permanent, despite opposition from local sheep farmers whose pasturage on the ancient common land was thus considerably shrunken.

Conversely, Robert Kennedy, Honorary Secretary of the Kildare Hunt, was delighted by the unexpected arrival of such a ready and constant source of well-educated, horse-savvy officers willing to contribute to the hunt coffers. Likewise, for the Mrs Bennets of County Kildare, with daughters to marry, the prospect of so many eligible and dashing young Englishmen on their doorsteps must have seemed like Manna from Heaven. Inspired by the presence of these military young bloods, a golden age of polo, cricket, tennis, racing and shooting parties enveloped the county. That said, these prospective brides sometimes had to compete for favours with a group of ladies known as the Curragh wrens, whose remarkable connection with the House of Windsor follows.

31 The Prince of Wales & the Curragh Wren

 On 3 July 1861, the twenty-year-old Prince of Wales (later Edward VII) commenced a ten-week sojourn at the Curragh Camp in County Kildare. As the eldest son of Queen Victoria and Prince Albert, 'Bertie' had a reputation as a wild and free-spirited youth. As such, his parents had dispatched him to 'the short grass' of the Curragh to spend some time with the Grenadier Guards in order that he might learn the essence of discipline. The Grenadiers were, after all, the most senior infantry regiment in the British Army. Despite a day of 'deplorable' weather, Bertie's parents must have had high hopes when they visited the Curragh on 23 August to watch their son parade.

And yet, in the mess, there was some rather more jocular talk among the Prince's fellow officers about his sheltered upbringing and his sacred virginity. It was inevitable that someone would suggest a union with one of the 'Curragh wrens'. That was the name given to an extraordinary harem of perhaps a hundred

women, mostly aged between seventeen and twenty-five, who lived amid the gorse-furze near the camp. Many had been orphaned by the Great Hunger that desecrated Ireland during their childhood. Bereft of options, they had turned to prostitution and made their way to the Curragh Camp, the biggest army barracks in Ireland, where they earned a meagre living by bestowing sexual gratification on the officers and soldiers.

The soldiers called them 'wrens' because their homes looked like nests, each abode stitched into the dense gorse that ran just a few hundred metres from the entrance to the camp. It was the only ground cover on the Curragh plain. James Greenwood, a reporter for the *Pall Mall Gazette*, visited the Curragh in 1867 and observed how each nest was 'no bigger than an ox's crib', perhaps 2.75 m (9 ft) long and 2 m (7 ft) broad. The roofs, for want of a better word, were not much more than 1.2 m (4 ft) high. They had no windows or chimneys, but the walls were impressive, 6 m (20 ft) thick in places, a closely compacted mesh of bog earth and gorse branches, that displayed 'not only certain signs of man's constructive skill, but of woman's occupancy...suspended against the prickly sides of one of them was a petticoat, against another a crinoline'.

Among the Curragh wrens was a good-humoured young woman named Nellie Clifden, considered by many officers to be the pick of the crop. Some say she was from Connemara in County Galway, but nobody knows how or why she ended up at the Curragh. Perhaps she came in with a soldier who had since died or abandoned her. James Greenwood interviewed one of her fellow wrens whose life story began with 'no mother, no father' and an aunt who kept a whiskey store in Cork City. One day an artilleryman had come into the whiskey store and, by and by, the girl became pregnant. When his regiment was posted to the

Curragh, she followed him. Some years later, she told Green-wood how the soldier wanted no more to do with her after their arrival. 'He told me to come here instead,' she said, 'and do like the other women did. And what could I do? My child was born here, in this very place. And glad I was of the shelter, and glad I was when the child died – thank the blessed Mary! What could I do with a child?'

Perhaps, like most wrens, Nellie simply considered prostitution to be a reasonable livelihood, in which case the Curragh, with its vast number of men, was an eminently sensible place to be. All of the girls Greenwood met agreed that life in the furze was far preferable to the alternative horrors of the workhouse in Naas. Maybe she was the 'Ellen Clifton' who was baptized in the Catholic parish of Abbeyside, near Dungravan, County Waterford, in 1844, which would have made her seventeen years of age on that autumnal day when she strolled through the tumbling Kildare rains to meet the Prince of Wales. In many gentlemen's clubs and stately mansions across Ireland and Britain, Nellie Clifden was about to become rather a well-known name.

One can but imagine how or where the seduction played out. After some obligatory small talk, did she simply draw him towards her and begin unbuttoning his uniform? Did she wonder at the Grenadiers' motto, embossed upon each button, which stated *Honi soit qui mal y pense* ('Evil be to him who evil thinks'). In any event, the Prince lost his virginity at the Curragh of Kildare and the young man enjoyed himself so much that three nights later, Nellie was summoned back. The following night, he wrote 'NC, third time' in his diary.

Bertie was evidently much taken by Nellie. However, not all Grenadiers could keep a secret and news of this 'most disreputable liaison' soon leaked all the way into the ears of Baron

Stockmar, Prince Albert's most trusted advisor. Sensitive to Albert's revulsion of all things sexual, the Baron provided Albert with an edited version of his son's misdemeanours. Posterity would record Nellie as an 'actress'; Stockmar certainly made no mention of prostitution or Curragh wrens.

Already ailing from overwork and gastric disorder, Albert took the news of his son's dalliance badly. 'I knew that you were thoughtless and weak,' he wrote, 'but I could not think you depraved!' His greatest horror was that the Irish girl would become pregnant and file a paternity suit against the Prince, thereby destroying his son's chances of securing a wealthy European bride. 'If you were to try and deny it,' he added despairingly, 'she can drag you into a Court of Law to force you to own it and there with you (the Prince of Wales) in the witness box, she will be able to give before a greedy Multitude disgusting details of your profligacy for the sake of convincing the Jury; yourself cross-examined by a railing indecent attorney and hooted and yelled at by a Lawless Mob!! Oh, horrible prospect, which this person has in her power, any day to realise! And to break your poor parents' heart.'

General Robert Bruce, the Prince's governor, was assigned to act as the go-between for father and son; Bertie was instructed to supply the general with 'even the most trifling circumstance' of his 'evil deed' with Nellie. Bertie confessed and apologized, but he refused to name the officers who had landed him in the soup. When Albert broke the news to Victoria, he spared her the 'disgusting details'. The royal couple agreed that, first and foremost, an early marriage was now essential or the Prince would be 'lost'. Within three weeks of 'NC, third time', Bertie was plucked from the Curragh and shipped to Germany where he was introduced to Princess Alexandra of Denmark who Albert and Victoria had determined to be his wife. He was then enrolled at Cambridge University and placed under constant surveillance.

The entire affair might have blown over but for Albert's decision to visit his wayward son in Cambridge. *'Bin recht elend'* ('I feel miserable'), he complained to his diary the day before they met. It was an emotional rain-swept encounter in which he forgave his son, but just three weeks later Albert was dead. Contemporaries attributed his demise to typhoid fever. Modern scholars believe it was most likely stomach cancer. However, for the grief-stricken Queen Victoria, it was quite clear that her beloved husband had died because of his shock at learning of the carnal night, or nights, that their firstborn son had spent with Nellie Clifden. 'I never can or shall look at him without a shudder,' she wrote of Bertie. For the rest of her life, she openly and repeatedly treated her heir with utter contempt.

More than four decades after his three-night fling with Nellie Clifden, Edward VII, King of the United Kingdom and the British Dominions, and Emperor of India, returned to visit the Curragh with Queen Alexandra by his side. As his carriage rumbled through the grassy plains of Kildare, the corpulent playboy must have reminisced with mixed emotions.

As to Nellie, her fate remains a mystery. Was she paid off by the royal family? Did she change her name and go on to greater things? Or, when the Prince's lust was spent, did she simply return to the Curragh furze and solicit further shillings from passing soldiers? In any event, aside from a popular racing mare cheekily named 'Miss Clifden' by one of Bertie's friends, her name and life story would vanish from the archives without trace.

32 John Henry Foley, Sculptor of an Empire

 Among those gathered in Dublin's Phoenix Park to watch the Duke of Marlborough perform his duties as viceroy of Ireland on an autumnal day in 1878 was his four-year-old grandson, Winston Churchill. Decades later, Churchill would recall how the Duke pulled off 'the brown shiny sheet' to reveal a splendid new equestrian statue to Field Marshal Sir Hugh Gough. 'An illustrious Irishman' declared the legend beneath Gough's name, along with details of his victories in China and the Punjab where, as the Duke reminded his listeners, 'with a withering volley he shattered the enemy's line'.

Gough's bronze memorial would remain on that very spot for just short of eighty years, despite half a dozen attempts to destroy him. However, on the sixth strike in 1957, a splinter group of radicals blew him off his perch with dynamite. As the Dublin poet Vincent Caprani put it in his bawdy 'Ballad of Gough':

For this is the way our 'hay-roes' today,
Are challenging England's might,
With a stab in the back and a midnight attack,
On a horse that can't even shite.

The various parts of both Gough and his horse survived and, Humpty Dumpty-like, he was soldered together again. In 1986 the reconstructed statue was spirited out of the country for safe-keeping and he now stands proud if forlorn in the grounds of Chillingham Castle in Northumberland, England.

Gough's statue was the work of John Henry Foley, probably the most influential sculptor in Irish history. He was born in the shadow of Dublin's Custom House on what is now called Foley Street in his honour; known as Montgomery Street at the time of his birth in 1818, it was populated by stonemasons and artisans building the new docks. It would later become notorious as 'the Monto', Dublin's red-light district.

Young Foley became hooked on sculpture watching his grandfather carve some of the riverine god headstones that still adorn the Custom House today. He advanced to the Royal Dublin Society's Drawing Schools at Leinster House where he quickly proved his genius. He was sent to the Royal Academy in London where he again excelled, catching the eye of Prince Albert, who became one of his patrons. In 1844 he won a contest to design two key figures for the new Houses of Parliament at Westminster. Thereafter he was never short of work again.

Foley's output was nothing less than staggering and included three equestrian statues of imperial British icons that were erected in the Maidan of Kolkata after the Indian Rebellion was crushed in 1857. He produced an immense number of works for Ireland. His troika of Oliver Goldsmith, Edmund Burke and

Henry Grattan still stand outside the front entrance to Trinity College Dublin. At the Royal College of Physicians in Dublin, three past presidents gaze sternly at those who pass before them. Sir Benjamin Lee Guinness, the brewing magnate, is immortalized in the grounds of St Patrick's Cathedral, the restoration of which he single-handedly financed. Foley also carved the statues of the astronomy-loving 3rd Earl of Rosse in Birr, County Offaly, and of Father Theobald Mathew in Cork. Known as the Apostle of Temperance, Father Mathew somehow persuaded half the adult population of Ireland to swear off alcohol in the 1840s.

Towards the end of Foley's life, Queen Victoria called into his studio and requested that he create the 10-tonne bronze statue of her beloved husband that now sits beneath his starry canopy at the Albert Memorial in London. The Dublin-born sculptor died, exhausted, aged fifty-six, in 1874. Victoria decreed that he be buried in St Paul's Cathedral, London. At the time of his death, there were a dozen statues at his Islington studio, mostly incomplete, including Prince Albert, the Confederate general Thomas 'Stonewall' Jackson (now in Richmond, Virginia) and Daniel O'Connell, which was unveiled on O'Connell Street, Dublin, in 1882.

Foley's statue to Field Marshal Gough was not the only one to be attacked. Indeed, the sculptor was still alive when unknown persons tried to destroy two of his Dublin-based works on a single night in June 1872. Gunpowder was placed around the base of his Prince Albert statue, which stood outside Leinster House. At the People's Garden in Phoenix Park, a rocket was fired at his statue of Lord Carlisle, one of Ireland's more popular viceroys. Neither attempt was successful. Prince Albert remained where he was until the birth of the Irish Free State. Leinster House had by then become Dáil Éireann, the seat of the Irish Parliament, and a monument to Queen Victoria's husband at the centre of the lawn was deemed inappropriate. He was shovelled off to one side, where he stands unobtrusively to this day, despite a 2018 petition to have him entirely ejected from the site.

However, a statue of Queen Victoria by John Hughes, which also used to stand outside Leinster House, proved too much and was subsequently shipped off to Australia. She had a better fate than her royal predecessors – a statue of William of Orange was removed from College Green after a bomb attack on Armistice Day 1929, while George II was blown sky-high by an explosion that coincided with the Coronation of George VI in 1937.

Foley's Lord Carlisle finally met his maker in 1958, with another attack, almost a year after Gough was destroyed. Nelson's Pillar on O'Connell Street survived the Easter Rising of 1916, although a rebel marksman managed to take off some of the admiral's nose. However, as Dublin prepared to mark the 50th anniversary of the Rising in 1966, the statue was blown off its perch by a radical group; the explosion also destroyed the upper part of the fine Doric pillar beneath and the Irish army were summoned to remove its stump. Nelson's head is now on display in the Dublin City Library and Archive in Pearse Street, while the site of the pillar has been occupied by the Spire of Dublin since 2003.

It was not only nationalists who considered statues fair game. Foley's 4.3-m (14-ft)-high O'Connell Monument in Dublin was used as target practice by British soldiers during the Rising, while loyalists bombed it in 1969. Two years later, loyalists also took out Edward Delaney's 1967 statue of Wolfe Tone, the nationalist icon, at St Stephen's Green; dubbed 'Tonehenge', it was subsequently rebuilt.

Or spare a thought for Foley's larger-than-life-sized statue of Lord Dunkellin, a brother of one of Galway's biggest landowners. In 1922, supporters of the short-lived Galway Soviet threw a rope around his neck, hauled him to the seaside and threw him in the water. As the statue sank, the band played 'I'm Forever Blowing Bubbles'.

33 Bloody Balfour's Kindly Deeds

 He would be remembered in nationalist lore as 'Bloody Balfour', the man whose tenure as Chief Secretary of Ireland between 1887 and 1891 was marred by a fresh wave of rural violence, including the 'Mitchelstown Massacre', in which police opened fire on an unarmed crowd, killing three. And yet of the 130 or so men who occupied the office of Chief Secretary between 1566 and 1922, this shy, aloof and rather prissy bachelor arguably made more of an impact on the Irish landscape than any of them.

Born in Scotland in 1848, Arthur Balfour was named after his godfather, Arthur Wellesley, the Duke of Wellington. Educated at Eton and Cambridge, he seemed destined for academia until his election as Conservative Member of Parliament for Hertford in 1874. Seven years later, his career prospects were greatly boosted when his mother's brother Robert Cecil, 3rd Marquess of Salisbury, succeeded the late Benjamin Disraeli to become head of the Conservative Party.

Balfour was appointed his uncle's private secretary shortly before Salisbury became prime minister of the United Kingdom in 1885. Two years later, Salisbury invited his imperialist nephew to Dublin Castle to take up office as Chief Secretary on a handsome annual salary of £4,500, equivalent to about £550,000 today, thus giving rise to the expression, 'Bob's your uncle'.

A fierce opponent of Home Rule, Balfour's determination to wipe out Irish nationalism led to the no-nonsense Coercion Act of 1887, which outlawed boycotting, intimidation, unlawful assembly and 'conspiracies against the payment of rents'. However, while Balfour believed coercion would eliminate the symptoms of nationalism, he also wanted to treat the causes. He toured the island extensively and made a detailed study of the works of James Hack Tuke, an elderly Quaker philanthropist, who had devoted his life to trying to remedy the ills of the west of Ireland. Balfour then instigated a policy that would become known as 'Constructive Unionism'.

It was Balfour's opinion that nationalism was, to quote W. B. Yeats, 'born in the peasant's cot, where men forgive if the belly gain'. He recognized that the vast majority of Irish people were at best apathetic and mostly opposed to the idea of self-government. His conclusion was that many Irishmen had become revolutionary simply because they had nothing else to do. He was also concerned by the continuing overdependence of so many people on the ever-vulnerable potato; crop failures, including a blight in 1890, frequently threatened widespread distress.

In 1891, Chief Secretary Balfour established the Congested Districts Board (CDB), a pioneering regional planning agency that was given sweeping powers to stimulate agriculture and local industry in the poorer, forgotten parts of Ireland. Its initial remit was the counties along the Atlantic shore from Donegal to West

Cork, where there was little more than bog and stone for its pre-dominantly Irish-speaking population to work with. It is unlikely that Balfour was an enthusiast for the Irish language but it was certainly a telling sign of how badly these communities had suffered from emigration when only 14.5 per cent of the population were clocked as Irish speakers in the 1891 census.

Following a thorough survey of the terrain, the CDB launched a remarkably ambitious array of projects. Its determination to stimulate the fishing industry resulted in the greatest era of pier-building in Irish history, including the £10,000 pier at Killybegs harbour in County Donegal, where the letters 'C.D.B.' are still emblazoned on a nearby rock. All told, 128 marine works were completed by 1900 as new and improved piers, quays, boat slips and landing places, as well as beacons and lighthouses,

sprang up all along the west coast. The CDB invested in boat-building, particularly the two-masted 'Zulu' fishing boats, but also traditional Irish currachs and hookers, as well as equipment for the fishing communities. It also paid for the construction of twenty fish-curing stations. With the coming of the railways, fishermen could now export creel after creel of fresh mackerel, herring and lobster by train all the way to Dublin and beyond.

Elsewhere the CDB paid for the construction of bridges and new roads, as well as drainage schemes and fencing. However, its most visible legacy was the railway, which was to enjoy a golden age in Balfour's time, just before the 'horseless carriage' motored into the plot and changed everything. Under the CDB, Ireland's railway network was radically extended as over 16,000 men set to work laying fifteen new lines leading into these often

difficult and sparsely populated parts. The cost was immense, at one point hitting the present-day equivalent of about £310,000 per km (£500,000 per mile). A huge viaduct leapt across the estuary at Ballydehob to bring the Schull & Skibbereen Railway into West Cork. Another carried the Connemara railway across the River Corrib from Galway City. When those locomotives first began chugging into places like Donegal, Mayo, Connemara, West Clare and Kerry, it was clear that Balfour had opened up the west like never before. In 1894, the quickest way to complete the 79-km (49-mile) journey from Galway to Clifden involved eight long hours squashed inside a Bianconi coach. When the Connemara railway opened on New Year's Day, 1895, it cut the travel time to two and a half hours.

The CDB also subsidized local crafts and cottage industries such as lacemaking, handloom weaving, knitting, tweed and carpet making, as well as beekeeping. By the early 1900s, the Killybegs carpet factory employed over six hundred women, while both Liberty and Debenhams of London were stocking Donegal lace. A number of these weavers, lacemakers, spinners and woodcarvers were to gain international attention at the 'Irish Village' exhibition in the Chicago Columbian Exposition of 1893.

In its bid to enrich the quality of farming in congested areas, the CDB brought in agricultural experts to advise on the raising of crops and livestock. It also supplied aspiring farmers with improved seed, manure and trees. Over £60,000 was expended on refining breeds of workhorses and donkeys at a farm in Stillorgan, then a village outside Dublin; the CDB also introduced the Spanish jackass, adroitly nicknamed the 'congested ass'. Hundreds of Aberdeen Angus, Galloway, Red and Shorthorn cattle were sent west to stock the new farms. For possibly the first time in history, landlords themselves were making a concerted effort to improve both their lands *and* the welfare of those who lived on them. Such initiatives inspired an Irish-born Wyoming rancher named Horace Plunkett to return home and establish the cooperative dairies in 1894, setting in motion the high standards that Irish dairy produce continues to hold to this day.

Landownership was of pivotal importance to Balfour, who believed that Irishmen of wavering loyalty could be won back to the empire if they were given their own stake in the soil. To this end, he ignited a major shake-up by investing almost £14 million in the purchase of land – primarily uneconomic small-holdings – which were then amalgamated and resold to tenants. By 1896, some 47,000 people had been given loans to buy their own land.

By 1910, the CDB's geographic remit had doubled so that it now exercised influence over a third of the country and a quarter of its population. Likewise, its original annual budget of £41,000, drawn from Church of Ireland funds, had mushroomed into a Treasury-supported £530,000 by 1912. The CDB's readiness to spend made it understandably popular but many eyebrows were raised by its consistent levels of mismanagement and profligacy.

Arthur Balfour's younger brother Gerald served as Chief Secretary of Ireland from 1895 to 1900. It was he who confessed that 'the government would, of course, be very glad if they were able by kindness to kill Home Rule'. In truth, there was not a huge amount to kill at that time. Arthur had taken office shortly after the defeat of the first Home Rule bill, which had caused Britain's ruling Liberal Party to split in two. In 1890, to Balfour's delight, Charles Stewart Parnell, Ireland's most powerful advocate for Home Rule, was completely destroyed by revelations of an adulterous love affair with the wife of one of his deputies. The rejection of a second Home Rule bill in 1893 left the

Conservatives with free rein to do pretty much whatever they wanted for the next decade.

That said, it was a political crisis that compelled Gerald Balfour to hastily introduce the Local Government Act of 1898, a reform that unintentionally did more for Irish nationalism than almost anything else. At a stroke, the unelected, landlord-dominated grand juries of old were replaced with democratically elected county councils and rural district councils in which nationalists finally had an opportunity to exert some power at local level.

In 1902, Arthur Balfour became Britain's prime minister. The passage of the Wyndham Land Act the following year was a green light for the CDB to start buying up as much land as possible from Irish landlords. By this means, the CDB purchased upwards of a thousand estates, containing almost 60,000 holdings. It had acquired over 809,000 hectares (2 million acres) by the time it was absorbed into the Land Commission when the new Irish Free State took shape in 1923.

Meanwhile, Balfour's initiatives were bearing fruit. Seaside resorts sprang up in places such as Mulranny in County Mayo, Kilrush in County Clare and 'Breezy Bundoran' (the 'Brighton of Ireland') in County Donegal, while scores of gentry and aristocracy were leaping onto westward-bound trains armed with fishing rods, shotguns and fat wallets, eager to enjoy this wild, unknown landscape of remote rivers and snipe bogs. The opening of the West Clare Railway generated a useful income among women selling butter and eggs; they spent part of their profits on new concertinas, or squeezy boxes, a craze that revived the county's deep love for traditional music. With London restaurants now serving Irish lobster, the Balfour brothers could be forgiven for thinking that they had won, that their entrepreneurial zest had sapped Irish nationalism of its anger and that the disparate voices would soon be reconciled to the glories of British rule.

However, for all the ghillies and fishermen who benefited from Balfour's project, there was a flip side. The railway also offered inhabitants of those hitherto isolated places a way out, an opportunity to board a train and start anew elsewhere. Within a very short time, the people themselves had become much the biggest export to be carried along the tracks. In turn, the dwindling population made the lines untenable, which is why most of them subsequently closed. The railway tracks for the Connemara line were sold to a German scrap merchant in 1938; the cut-stone columns of the Corrib viaduct are still visible today.

The closure of the railway line from Westport to Achill Island in County Mayo was particularly eerie. In 1894, the very first locomotive to reach the island had been a special train laid on to carry the bodies of thirty islanders who drowned in Clew Bay while making their way by sea to Scotland. Forty-three years later, another train arrived into Achill with the bodies of another ten young islanders who had been killed in a cabin fire near Glasgow. The Achill railway closed two weeks later, thus fulfilling a prophecy by Brian Rua Ó Ceabháin, a 17th-century mountain farmer from northern Mayo, who apparently predicted that 'carriages on wheels with smoke and fire will come to Achill, and the first and last carriages will carry dead bodies'.

34 Queen Victoria's Dublin Visit, 1900

In April 1900, Queen Victoria stunned her closest advisors when she announced her intention of visiting Ireland for the first time in nearly forty years. The Queen was known to be deeply uneasy about the Irish. In 1849, while heavily pregnant with her seventh child, she narrowly avoided being assassinated by a farm labourer from Adare, County Limerick. Two decades later, a Dubliner shot and wounded her son Alfred in Australia. She was also profoundly upset when Fenians attempted to blow up a statue of her beloved husband, Prince Albert, outside Leinster House (see chapter 32). Nonetheless, the eighty-one-year-old widow had already cancelled her traditional springtime visit to the French Riviera and set her sights on an informal sojourn in Dublin. It was, she said, her own idea; the Irish capital would be good for her health.

With just three weeks to prepare, there were plenty of headaches for the organizers. Many predicted that the royal visit would be a disaster, not least with Irish public opinion swinging rapidly against the British Empire in the wake of newspaper accounts of the brutal treatment of Boer women and children in the Anglo-Boer War in South Africa. In 1899, the actress Maud Gonne and Arthur Griffith, editor of the *United Irishman*, a nationalist newspaper, had co-founded the Irish Transvaal Committee. In the months prior to the Queen's visit they held a series of pro-Boer rallies in Dublin, leading to a notable decline in the numbers volunteering for armed service. To counter such negative press, two days before her arrival in Dublin, Victoria formally created a new regiment, the Irish Guards, in honour of the thousands of Irishmen already serving in the war.

The royal yacht sailed for Ireland on the 100th anniversary of the Act of Union and dropped anchor in the harbour at Kingstown (present-day Dún Laoghaire) at 2.15 p.m. on 3 April. At that precise moment, one hundred cannons boomed out across Dublin Bay. The high standard of the vessels that greeted the Queen was something of an illusion; the harbour had been deliberately filled with 'better-class yachts' ahead of her visit. Everything had to be just so. The drivers of the Kingstown train were instructed to 'minimize the whistling of the engines and the noise from shunting'. The mailboats in the harbour were requested to refrain from sounding their steam horns 'except in cases of absolute necessity'. Security was also tight: every berth in the harbour had been 'examined by divers'.

As the Queen slept on her yacht that first night, the sky over Dublin exploded into the greatest fireworks display the city had seen. The following morning, she stepped on shore at Kingstown and was ushered into a purpose-built pavilion to meet the first of many dignitaries. She then set off in a convoy of four royal carriages on a 14.5-km (9-mile) journey to Phoenix Park, passing through 'endless streets full of enthusiastic people', as she marvelled in her diary.

The royal visit was all about giving Dublin – and Dubliners – a sense of imperial identity, to make sure that every onlooker felt a part of this British-led world order and that the little old woman in the royal carriage was not just the Queen but *their* queen. As such, the councils on the south side went to tremendous expense and effort to ensure their area was shipshape. Bunting criss-crossed every street. Union Jacks fluttered on rooftops and gates. Royal mottoes and emblems graced every pedestal and pillar. Multicoloured bulbs were strewn across banks and factories. And all along the way, huge crowds gathered to watch and cheer, to wave scarves and handkerchiefs and throw their hats in the air.

It was, *The Times* claimed, 'a display of loyalty absolutely unparalleled in the records of public rejoicing', with marching bands and hundreds of scarlet-dressed mounted cavalry adding to the sense of occasion. By night, the streets were lit up by electricity and gas like never before. Many leading citizens rented special electrical tramcars so they could tour the city after dusk and behold the illuminations.

Not everyone was in favour of all this pomp. Many nationalists agreed with Maud Gonne's assertion that the only reason Victoria had taken 'a shamrock into her withered hand' was to stimulate the recruitment of Irish soldiers into the British Army. Others questioned why the Queen was not shown the city's north side, where upwards of 200,000 slum dwellers were living in abject poverty.

Inevitably, there was a large increase in the military and police presence on the streets. There was to be zero tolerance for protests, particularly from the Irish Transvaal Committee. When

Gonne and her supporters gathered for a torchlight procession on the night the Queen reached Dublin, they were charged down by baton-wielding policemen and sent fleeing. The following day, the *United Irishman* published an article by Gonne, entitled 'The Famine Queen', in which she castigated the 'vile and selfish' monarch for presiding over an 'organised famine'. The police seized most copies of the paper during an early morning raid on Griffith's office. As an indirect consequence, Griffith, the future founder of Sinn Féin, was sentenced to two weeks' imprisonment.

Dublin Corporation also posed a problem. Nearly half its members opposed the visit, including James Egan, a lifelong Fenian, to whom the Corporation had entrusted the civic sword; he refused to present it to the Queen and resigned. Like Gonne, these more militant nationalists were convinced the 'private' visit was a recruitment drive.

Thomas Devereux Pile, the Lord Mayor of Dublin, headed up the moderate nationalists and managed to secure a majority in favour of greeting the Queen. He duly presented her with the civic sword, the ancient city keys and 'a most hearty welcome' when they met beneath a hastily constructed 21-m (70-ft)-high timber tower by Leeson Street Bridge, which served as the 'entrance' to the city. Pile was subsequently elevated to the peerage as Baron Kenilworth.

For the next twenty nights, Victoria stayed at the Vice-Regal Lodge, riding around Phoenix Park in a pony-chair most days, smiling and sporting sunglasses, attending military reviews and visiting a series of schools, convents, hospitals, churches and aristocratic mansions in between. On 7 April, she attended a 'Children's Day' in Phoenix Park where 52,000 children were given sandwiches, biscuits and fruit. The following July, Maud Gonne and the pro-Boer Inghinidhe na hÉireann (Daughters of

Ireland) retaliated by organizing a 'Patriotic Children's Treat' in Clonturk Park attended by nearly 30,000 children whom Gonne addressed, urging them to never take a job in the British Army.

For monarchy and imperialism, the Queen's three-week visit was a massive publicity success, despite the odds, not unlike Queen Elizabeth II's historic visit to the Republic of Ireland in 2011. The *Freeman's Journal* was not alone in admiring 'the pluck of the little old lady' who had 'conquered her repugnance towards Ireland in order to put in a stroke for her Army, her Empire and her Throne'.

Victoria departed from Kingstown in glorious sunshine on 26 April, with loyal Abdul Karim, her turbaned Indian attendant, by her side and a large bunch of shamrocks on her breast. To Lord Mayor Pile she said, 'I am very sorry to leave Ireland. I have had an extremely pleasant time.'

She died less than a year later, on 22 January 1901.

35 Killer Gas in the Great War

 On Thursday, 27 April 1916, Dubliners were awoken by gunfire on what was by then the fourth day of the Easter Rising, an insurrection that would leave 485 people dead, the majority of them civilians. Meanwhile, some 900 km (550 miles) southeast of Dublin, a number of Irish battalions were already several hours into what was to be their grimmest day yet on the Western Front, with over five hundred Irishmen killed.

Just under a thousand soldiers from the Royal Dublin Fusiliers were packed tight into the front-line trenches that ran alongside the Hulluch chalk pit in northern France. They had been contending with an intense bombardment of incendiary shells and tear-gas bombs since 4 a.m. when, with mounting horror, their commanding officer, Edward Bellingham, espied 'a dense cloud of black gas and smoke between us and the sun'.

The Germans had directed the contents of 3,800 cylinders of Grünkreuz gas, a deadly mix of phosgene and chlorine, at the

Irish lines. As it wafted westwards towards the Irish-held trenches, carried on the early morning breeze, British air patrols observed how it killed all the vegetation it passed over, 'down to the last blade of grass'. When the gas alarm was raised, the Dubs swiftly pulled on their canvas masks but many respirators were broken and many more were missing.

Further up the line, the 7th Battalion of the Royal Inniskilling Fusiliers were in precisely the same predicament. Private Tom Cassidy of Irvinestown, County Fermanagh, had not even had time to put on his socks. He accidentally put his sack-mask on the wrong way around and spent several precious minutes bumping around the trench in his bare feet. 'I wish I could find the bloody windows!' he yelled. Meanwhile, as the gas rolled ever closer, the men could do nothing but hope that it would miraculously drift over their heads. It didn't.

The poisonous gas engulfed the trenches and in moments those without effective gas masks were desperately battling for their lives. Some were instantly blinded, others hideously choked and suffocated. The trenches were soon full of retching and dying men, their faces a pallid green. The survivors were then faced with an equally ghastly sight of German troops, bayonets outstretched, pouring into the trenches to engage the bloodshot Irishmen in brutal hand-to-hand combat: 570 soldiers from the 16th (Irish) Division died, 338 killed by gas, 232 torn apart by shells and bayonets. The sockless Tom Cassidy was among the slain. A further 1,410 men were wounded, while at least 500 Germans are also thought to have perished.

The gas attack on the Irish trenches at Hulluch marked one of the many low points of the Great War in which the participants broke the terms of the 1907 Hague Convention and used 'asphyxiating or deleterious gases' to try and overwhelm the enemy.

Three days later, the Germans launched a second and even more severe gas attack on the Allied lines. On that occasion, they briefly broke through and took an unspecified number of prisoners but then the wind changed and blew the gas back into the Germans' faces, forcing them to retreat.

Over a third of Bellingham's battalion were killed, maimed or lost that week but, as he wrote in his journal, the Germans 'were put out again and the line held for the rest of the day by the remnants'. Among the dead was John Naylor, a private who had served as a porter at a grocery shop in Dublin before the war. In an astonishing twist, it would emerge that his wife, Margaret, had been shot while crossing Ringsend drawbridge in Dublin during the Easter Rising that very same day. Margaret, who died two days later, had been on a mission to fetch bread for their three, now so cruelly orphaned, daughters.

Also dead was Private Jack Weafer, a bricklayer and swimming enthusiast from Glasthule in Dublin, whose cousin Tom Weafer was shot dead on Dublin's Lower Abbey Street on 26 April while wearing the uniform of the rebel Irish Volunteers.

Fr Willie Doyle, a celebrated Jesuit chaplain, was on hand to perform the last rites and oversee the burials for many of the Hulluch dead. 'There they lay,' he recounted in a letter to his father, 'scores of them…in the bottom of the trench, in every conceivable posture of human agony; the clothes torn off their bodies in a vain effort to breathe, while from end to end of that valley of death came one low unceasing moan from the lips of brave men fighting and struggling for life. I don't think you will blame me when I tell you that, more than once, the words of Absolution stuck in my throat, and the tears splashed down on the patient, suffering faces of my poor boys, as I leant down to anoint them.'

36 Operation Shamrock

 On 27 July 1946, nine-year-old Herbert Remmel disembarked from the mailboat at the port of Dún Laoghaire in County Dublin and walked trance-like into the dense crowds gathered to greet him and the eighty-seven skinny and bewildered little boys and girls who had travelled with him. As he was hugged and petted and treated to mugs of cocoa and thick buttery sandwiches and fruits he had never seen before, Herbert marvelled that it was only seventy-two hours since he had said farewell to his parents amid the smouldering ruins of his native city, Cologne, in Germany. Overwhelmed by the occasion, he picked up an orange and sank his teeth into it. Peeling an orange was one of many useful skills this child of Nazi Germany would master in the post-war Republic of Ireland.

Remmel was one of over four hundred German children brought to Ireland under an Irish Red Cross initiative called 'Operation Shamrock'. Also known as 'Hitler's Irish Orphans', these children were primarily German Catholics from the province of North Rhine Westphalia. In most cases, their parents had been killed and their homes destroyed during the war.

Few German cities suffered more than Cologne, on which the Royal Air Force launched 262 air raids, reaching a crescendo on the night of 30/31 May 1942 when over a thousand planes struck, dropping a new bomb every other second for an hour and a half. Miraculously, the city's splendid twin-spired Gothic cathedral survived but the city itself was annihilated and, by the close of the war, over 20,000 of its citizens had been killed. For children like Herbert, there was some consolation in searching through the rubble for parts of shot-down RAF bombers to play with – empty petrol tanks became canoes, strips of old tyre were converted into catapults.

Herbert Remmel – not Rommel, as he corrected a Customs officer – grew up in Neurath, a 1920s housing estate on Cologne's north side. It was a poor working-class neighbourhood, dubbed 'Little Moscow' on account of the high number of socialists in the area. His father, Christian Remmel, was a prominent Communist who helped many socialists, Jews and others to escape from Germany during the 1930s. In 1943, the family home was destroyed in an air raid; the Remmels were safely secured in a bunker at the time. The following year, Christian was betrayed, arrested and sentenced to death. A US tank squadron liberated him just twenty-four hours before he was due to be executed.

Exhausted, famished and recovering from both typhus and dysentery, Christian was desperately seeking to rebuild his family after the war when he heard of a new scheme operating out of Ireland. He plucked up an atlas and began pondering its implications, while his sons roared with laughter. The word *Ire* meant 'mad' in their Cologne dialect. Ireland – the Land of the Mad!

Could there really be such a place?

Ireland remained neutral during the Second World War, a policy that was championed by the veteran Republican statesman Éamon de Valera, whose government ruled the country from 1932 to 1948. Such a stance had alienated many of the fledgling state's potential allies on the Continent. Operation Shamrock would arguably mark the start of Ireland's journey back into European favour. Despite being one of the Continent's poorest countries, Ireland was among the first and, according to Remmel, the 'most generous', when it came to helping out Europe's war-ravaged countries. In the first year after the war, de Valera's government pumped £12 million into food, medicine and the deployment of doctors and nurses, homing in on those places that had been hardest hit. Much of Ireland's focus was on Germany. No other country in Europe was inclined to help the defeated Fatherland when it was down. However, Ireland had enjoyed strong pre-war links with Germany and, as such, it was not surprising that, with the Nazis defeated and the vengeful Russian army swarming through Germany, Irish eyes began to consider the plight of German children.

On 16 October 1945, at a public meeting at the Shelbourne Hotel, Dublin, the paediatrician Dr Kathleen Murphy founded the German Save the Children Society to bring traumatized children to Ireland to help them recover from the nightmare of the war. It was by no means an easy sell. The initial empathy for Dr Murphy's society was dissipated when, as Remmel puts it, nationalists and fascists 'latched on', viewing Ireland as a 'Teuton gene-bank' and the society as an 'initiative' to save German 'blood'. Unwilling to be associated with such out-of-vogue conceits, the Irish government and the Department of External Affairs punted the society in the direction of the Irish Red Cross.

In March 1946 the Irish Red Cross applied to the Allied Control Council (ACC) to bring one hundred German children to Ireland. The ACC members were Russia, France, the US and the UK, none of which felt a mercy mission for German children should be high on their agenda. The concept was particularly unpopular with the British, through whose territory these children would have to travel in order to reach Ireland. Nonetheless, the Irish Red Cross gradually courted and wooed the relevant dignitaries of church and state, including the UK's Council member Field Marshal Bernard Montgomery.

The request was finally approved and the first wave of Operation Shamrock's refugees arrived in Dún Laoghaire in July 1946, Remmel among them. By the end of June 1947, 462 children, aged between three and ten, were in Ireland: 421 were German, 403 of them brought in by the Red Cross and 18 directly by families.

Herbert qualified for Operation Shamrock by dint of a treble of facts: he was under ten years old, the Nazis had persecuted his father and he was a Catholic. Indeed, one of the conditions of the operation was that there should be four Catholics for every Protestant. That said, Catholicism was not something the Remmel household had been strict on during Herbert's childhood. Travelling on a double-decker around Dublin a few weeks later, he was astonished by the clockwork habit of the Irish passengers who tipped their hats and crossed themselves every time they passed a church.

For the first two months, Herbert was based in the Old Brewery at Castlebellingham Green, County Louth, where he was cared for by the Sisters of Mercy and treated by doctors, nurses and specialists. Suffering from scabies and other diseases, many of the children were completely unable to stomach the rich Irish diet. Once they were deemed healthy enough, the

youngsters were sent to the Red Cross Centre at St Kevin's, Glencree, County Wicklow, now the Centre for Peace and Reconciliation. Although a large number of children returned to Germany at this point, Remmel was among those who stayed on to be dispatched to a foster home.

His first foster family were the Cunninghams of Inchicore, Dublin, with whom he stayed until a British embargo on Irish coal in 1947 so reduced their income that they had to cut him loose. While in Dublin, Herbert was shocked at the poverty of the homeless he saw on the streets, which was unlike anything he had seen in Cologne. He subsequently went to live and work on the Nally farm in Ballinlough, County Mayo, for two years, describing this era as 'the happiest and most interesting in my childhood'. He went to school, learned to speak Irish (primarily rude words) and to imitate Michael O'Hehir, the brilliant hurling, Gaelic football and horse-racing commentator. He played hurling and handball and took his First Communion. He helped the Nallys stack turf, spread manure, gather potatoes and make hay.

By the end of 1949, most Shamrock children were back in Germany. Many, like Remmel, formed strong bonds with their foster families; about fifty remained in Ireland and married Irish partners. A fountain at St Stephen's Green in Dublin stands as a mark of German gratitude for the kindness that was Operation Shamrock. The contacts made through the scheme laid the groundwork for the first post-war trade with Germany, which, in turn, paved the way for Ireland's entry into the European Economic Community.

Epilogue:
The Power of Remembrance

Only take heed to thyself, and keep thy soul diligently,
lest thou forget the things which thine eyes have seen...

Deuteronomy 4:9

The Republic of Ireland is approaching the last stages of its Decade of Centenaries, a project to commemorate the long run of 'significant events' in Irish history that took place between 1912 and 1922. Among the commemorated highlights have been the sinking of the ships *Titanic, Lusitania* and RMS *Leinster*; the passage of the Home Rule bill; the 1913 strike and lockout; the outbreak and battles of the Great War; the Easter Rising and the War of Independence. As exercises in remembering go, it has been extraordinarily successful. Each event in turn has been thoroughly interrogated, flipped over, spun around and cross-examined once again.

It is too soon to say what the long-term impact of this re-evaluation will be but it has certainly reshaped how future generations will remember those ten momentous years. In pursuit of 'positive' stories, the Decade of Centenaries has also spawned another deeply exciting project: Trinity College Dublin's 'Beyond 2022: Ireland's Virtual Record Treasury'. This major reconstruction of the Public Record Office of Ireland archive is reassembling documentary collections thought lost forever when the Record Treasury at the Four Courts was destroyed by fire during the Civil War.

Another striking legacy of the Decade of Centenaries has been to make it okay, at last, to talk about family members who served in the Allied forces during the Great War and, to an extent, the Second World War. For many Irish households, the fact that a great-uncle or a grandfather had 'taken the King's shilling' was considered a matter of immense private shame or, at best, something to be wilfully forgotten, but then we began to remember the quarter of a million Irish men and women who served in the Great War and, more specifically, the 36,000 who died. We remembered the hideous battles on the Western Front and Gallipoli and all those forgotten fronts – Salonika, Serbia, East Africa, Palestine, the Sinai Peninsula, Mesopotamia. We remembered the poignant moments – the Christmas truce, the football matches and 'Silent Night, Stille Nacht' drifting on the winter winds from trench to trench. We remembered the nurses and orderlies contending with the daily horror of that mad war and, in time, with the Spanish influenza that killed more people than the war itself.

And in between all that, we remembered every step of the Easter Rising of 1916 and the renewed battle for independence that would engulf this small island. The upshot of all this remembrance is that we have created a much more nuanced and rational interpretation of Irish history, something that the events of this book add a new slant to.

I don't believe it is pure coincidence that the years since we began this fresh excavation of our past have also been ones in which Ireland has emerged as one of the most liberal, tolerant democracies on Earth. This evolution was by no means predictable. When Pope John Paul II came to the Republic of Ireland in 1979, a third of the population went to Dublin to hear him say Mass. Four decades on, all the certainties of that austere, no-nonsense Catholic state have vanished. The people voted for same sex marriage and to repeal one of the strictest abortion laws in the Western world. They declared themselves happy for their leaders to be gay, for their presidents and judges, and even their priests, to be women. Such changes have been echoed in the Irish economy, its politics and its improved relationship with the old enemy, England.

The past is, of course, every bit as divisive as the present and yet memory, intelligently applied, can help to create a more honest, more forgiving world. The coming decades are on course to produce an unbelievable amount of new information about our global history, gathered up by academics and archaeologists, genealogists and local historians, and a welter of ingenious, insatiable, individual sleuths. We read their findings online, share them on social media, tune into their podcasts and watch re-enactments and virtual reconstructions on our screens.

Yes, a lot of what we read and see and hear needs to be prudently grilled, and there is still so much that is forgotten, but I personally derive considerable cheer from knowing that with every passing second, people all over this planet are doing their part to help us remember.

Bibliography

Historical research is like a constant and thoroughly addictive jigsaw. One shifts and twists the pieces around and around until that satisfying click takes place, after which one moves on to the next piece. I salute the British News Archive, which has made trawling through newspaper archives such a joyous and fruitful experience, and much of what appears in these pages has been fished from the pages of newspapers such as the *Dublin Evening Post*, *Saunders's News-Letter*, the *Freeman's Journal*, the *Dublin Courier* and the *Irish Times*, as well as periodicals like the *Kerry Archaeological Magazine*, the *Proceedings of the Royal Irish Academy*, *Carloviana*, the *Irish Sword* and the *Journal of the County Kildare Archaeological Society*. I also give a nod to podcasts from Myles Dungan (*The History Show*), Patrick Geoghegan (*Talking History*), Fin Dwyer (irishhistorypodcast.ie), Zack Twamley (*When Diplomacy Fails*), Dan Snow (*History Hit*), Dan Carlin (*Hardcore History*), Melvyn Bragg (*In Our Time*), Stephen Fry (*Great Leap Years*) and BBC *History Extra*.

As well as the *Cambridge Dictionary of Irish Biography*, I would like to acknowledge the following sources, which have played a role in helping me sketch the tales in this book.

It Starts with a Bear

Byrne, R. P. et al., 'Insular Celtic population structure and genomic footprints of migration', *PLoS Genetics*, vol. 14, no. 1 (25 Jan. 2018)

Dowd, Marion, 'A remarkable cave discovery', *Archaeology Ireland*, vol. 30, no. 2 (Summer 2016), pp. 21–25

Driscoll, Killian, 'The early prehistory in the west of Ireland: Investigations into the social archaeology of the Mesolithic, west of the Shannon, Ireland', M. Litt. thesis, Department of Archaeology, National University of Ireland, Galway (Oct. 2006)

Smith, Christopher, *Late Stone Age Hunters of the British Isles* (London: Routledge, 1992)

Waddell, John, *The Prehistoric Archaeology of Ireland*, rev. edn (Dublin: Wordwell, 2010)

Woodman, Peter C., *Ireland's First Settlers: Time and the Mesolithic* (Oxford: Oxbow Books, 2015)

Neolithic Stargazers

Macintosh, Alison A., Pinhasi, Ron and Stock, Jay T., 'Prehistoric women's manual labor exceeded that of athletes through the first 5500 years of farming in Central Europe', *Science Advances*, vol. 3, no. 11 (29 Nov. 2017)

Sánchez-Quinto, Federico et al., 'Megalithic tombs in western and northern Neolithic Europe were linked to a kindred society', *Proceedings of the National Academy of Sciences* (May 2019)

Archaeological Survey online database (webgis.archaeology.ie/historicenvironment/)

Archaeology Ireland website (archaeologyireland.ie)

Megalithic Ireland website (www.megalithicireland.com)

Mythical Ireland website (www.mythicalireland.com)

The Bell Beakers

Burl, Aubrey, *The Stone Circles of Britain, Ireland and Brittany* (New Haven: Yale University Press, 2000)

Davies, Norman, *The Isles: A History* (London: Macmillan, 1999)

Flanagan, Laurence, *Ancient Ireland: Life before the Celts* (Dublin: Gill & Macmillan, 1998)

Harbison, Peter, *Pre-Christian Ireland: From the First Settlers to the Early Celts* (London: Thames & Hudson, 1994)

McCormick, Finbar, 'The horse in early Ireland', *Anthropozoologica*, vol. 42, no. 1 (2007), pp. 85–104

Ó Maoldúin, Ros, 'Exchange in Chalcolithic and Early Bronze Age (EBA) Ireland: Connecting people, objects and ideas', PhD thesis, Department of Archaeology, National University of Ireland, Galway (Aug. 2014)

Standish, C. D. et al., 'The genesis of gold mineralisation hosted by orogenic belts: A lead isotope investigation of Irish gold deposits', *Chemical Geology*, vols 378–79 (15 Jun. 2014), pp. 40–51

Waddell, John, *The Prehistoric Archaeology of Ireland*, rev. edn (Dublin: Wordwell, 2010)

Pagan Christians & Holy Wells

Branigan, Gary, *Ancient & Holy Wells of Dublin* (Dublin: The History Press, 2012)

Carroll, Michael P., *Irish Pilgrimage: Holy Wells and Popular Catholic Devotion* (Baltimore: Johns Hopkins University Press, 1999)

Celeste, Ray, *The Origins of Ireland's Holy Wells* (Oxford: Archaeopress Archaeology, 2014)

Croker, Thomas Crofton, *Researches in the South of Ireland* (London: John Murray, 1824)

Logan, Patrick, *The Holy Wells of Ireland* (Gerrards Cross: Colin Smythe, 1980)

McQuinn, Christopher, 'St. Fortchern – Patron of Tullow', *Carloviana* (2011)

Ancient & Holy Wells of Ireland Facebook Group

High Crosses of the Kingdom of Ossory

Harbison, Peter, *The High Crosses of Ireland* (Dublin: Royal Irish Academy, 1992)

Killanin, Lord and Duignan, Michael V., *The Shell Guide to Ireland* (London: Ebury Press & George Rainbird, 1967)

McGuire, James and Quinn, James (eds), *Dictionary of Irish Biography* (Dublin and Cambridge: Royal Irish Academy and Cambridge University Press, 2009)

Mitchell, Frank, et al., *Treasures of Early Irish Art: 1500 BC to 1500 AD* (New York: Metropolitan Museum of Art and Alfred A. Knopf, 1977)

The Uí Dúnlainge Kings of Leinster

Radner, Joan N. (ed. and trans.), *Fragmentary Annals of Ireland* (Dublin: Dublin Institute for Advanced Studies, 1978)

Sitric Silkbeard & Queen Gormflaith

Duffy, Seán, *Brian Boru and the Battle of Clontarf* (Dublin: Gill & Macmillan, 2014)

The Knights Templar of Ireland

Jones, Dan, *The Templars* (London: Head of Zeus, 2017)

Lord, Evelyn, *Knights Templar in Britain* (Abingdon: Routledge, 2013)

Mac Aodhagain, Sean, *Finding the Holy Grail* (Milton Keynes: AuthorHouse, 2009)

Nicholson, Helen J., 'The testimony of Brother Henry Danet and the trial of the Templars in Ireland', in Ronnie Ellenblum, Jonathan Riley-Smith and Iris Shagrir (eds), *In Laudem Hierosolymitani: Studies in Crusades and Medieval Culture in Honour of Benjamin Z. Kedar* (Abingdon: Routledge, 2016)

Walsh, Thomas, *History of the Irish Hierarchy: With the Monasteries of Each County, Biographical Notices of the Irish Saints, Prelates, and Religious* (New York: D. & J. Sadlier & Company, 1854)

Prince Lionel Comes to Carlow

Bunbury, Turtle, *Carlow 800: 800 Years of an Irish Castle* (Carlow: Carlow County Council, 2013)

Canny, Nicholas, *Making Ireland British 1580–1650* (Oxford: Oxford University Press, 2001)

Clarke, Aidan, *The Old English in Ireland 1625–42* (London: MacGibbon & Kee, 1966)

Dunn, Alastair, 'Thomas Holand – Richard II's King of Ireland?', *History of Ireland*, vol. 1, no. 1 (Spring 2003)

Gilbert, John T., 'Proceedings of the forces in Ireland under Sir Hardress Waller and Lord-Deputy Ireton by Parliamentary army officers 1650–1651', in Gilbert, *A Contemporary History of Affairs in Ireland*, vol. 3, part 2 (Dublin: Irish Archaeological Society, 1880), pp. 218–63 (see celt.ucc.ie for electronic text edn)

Jarvis, Ann M., 'Carlow material: Petworth House Archives', *Carlow Past and Present*, vol. 1, no. 4 (1993)

King, Thomas, *Carlow: The Manor and Town, 1674–1721*, Maynooth Studies in Local History, 12 (Dublin: Irish Academic Press, 1997)

Lenihan, Pádraig, *Confederate Catholics at War 1641–49* (Cork: Cork University Press, 2001)

Malcomson, Anthony P., *The Pursuit of the Heiress: Aristocratic Marriage in Ireland 1740–1840* (Belfast: Ulster Historical Foundation, 2006)

Great Pretenders & Warring Roses

Butler, George, 'The Battle of Piltown, 1462', *The Irish Sword*, vol. VI (1963–64), pp. 196–212

The Midland Shires

D'Alton, Edward Alfred, *History of Ireland: From the Earliest Times to the Present Day* (London: Gresham Publishing, 1903)

Sir William Stanley, Public Enemy No. 1

Whitelock, Anna, *Elizabeth's Bedfellows: An Intimate History of the Queen's Court* (London: Bloomsbury, 2013)

Rise & Fall: The Maguires of Fermanagh

Livingstone, Father Peadar, *A Fermanagh Story* (Enniskillen: Cumann Seanchais Chlochair, 1969)

Cromwell's Tailor

Byrne-Rothwell, Daniel, *The Byrnes and the O'Byrnes: Volume Two* (Isle of Colonsay: House of Lochar, 2010)

Gmerek, Katarzyna, 'Follow me up to Warsaw: A contribution to the history of the O'Byrnes in Poland', in Michael Hornsby and Karolina Rosiak (eds), *Eastern European Perspectives on Celtic Studies* (Newcastle upon Tyne: Cambridge Scholars Publishing, 2018), pp. 132–62

Ó Siochrú, Micheál, *God's Executioner: Oliver Cromwell and the Conquest of Ireland* (London: Faber & Faber, 2008)

The Byerley Turk: A Warhorse on the Boyne

Ahnert, Rainer L. (editor in chief), *Thoroughbred Breeding of the World* (Germany: Pozdun Publishing, 1970)

Gough, John, *A History of the People Called Quakers* (Dublin: Robert Jackson, 1790)

'Byerley, Robert (1660–1714)', in B. D. Henning (ed.), *The History of Parliament: The House of Commons 1660–1690* (London: Martin Secker & Warburg, 1983)

James, Jeremy, *The Byerley Turk: The True Story of the First Thoroughbred* (Ludlow: Merlin Unwin Books, 2007)

Whyte, James Christie, *History of the British Turf: From the Earliest Period to the Present Day, Volume I* (London: H. Colburn, 1840), p. 90

The Lixnaw Project

Knightly, John, 'Lixnaw and the earls of Kerry', *Journal of the Kerry Archaeological and Historical Society*, series 2, vol. 10 (2010)

Lyne, Gerard J., *The Lansdowne Estate in Kerry Under W. S. Trench, 1849–72* (Dublin: Geography Publications, 2001)

O'Kane, Finola, *Ireland and the Picturesque: Design, Landscape Painting and Tourism 1700–1840* (New Haven: Yale University Press, 2013)

Smith, Charles, MD, *The Ancient and Present State of the County of Kerry: Containing a Natural, Civil, Ecclesiastical, Historical and Topographical Description Thereof* (Dublin: 1774, first published 1756)

irishwaterwayshistory.com

Lord Rosse & the Hell-Fire Club

Chearnley, Samuel, *Miscelanea Structura Curiosa* (County Kerry: Churchill House Press, 2005)

Lord, Evelyn, *The Hell-Fire Clubs: Sex, Satanism and Secret Societies* (New Haven: Yale University Press, 2010)

Ryan, David, *Blasphemers & Blackguards: The Irish Hellfire Clubs* (County Kildare: Irish Academic Press, 2012)

Somerville-Large, Peter, *Irish Eccentrics: A Selection* (Dublin: Lilliput Press, 1975)

Peg Plunkett, Queen of Vice

Lyons, Mary (ed.), *The Memoirs of Mrs. Leeson, Madam* (Dublin: Lilliput Press, 1995)

Peakman, Julie, *Peg Plunkett: Memoirs of a Whore* (London: Quercus, 2015)

Gold Fever in Avoca

McArdle, Peadar, *Gold Frenzy: The Story of Wicklow's Gold* (Dublin: Albertine Kennedy Publishing, 2011)

O'Shea, Katherine, *The Uncrowned King of Ireland* (Stroud: The History Press, 2005)

Medicinal Springs

Foley, Ronan, *Healing Waters: Therapeutic Landscapes in Historic and Contemporary Ireland* (Abingdon: Routledge, 2016)

Hill, John, MD, *The Distinct Symptoms of the Gravel and Stone* (Dublin: James Hoey, 1760)

Lewis, Samuel, *A Topographical Dictionary of Ireland* (London: Lewis & Co, 1837)

Rutty, John, *An Essay towards the Natural History of the County of Dublin* (Dublin, 1772)

Wilson, William, *The Post-Chaise Companion: Or, Travellers Directory Through Ireland* (Dublin: J. Fleming, 1786)

The Crimean Banquet

Huddie, Paul. '"Removing some big guns": The story of Dublin's Crimean War trophy guns from 1857 to the present', *Dublin Historical Record*, vol. 67, no. 1 (2014), pp. 6–18

Murphy, David, *Ireland and the Crimean War* (Dublin: Four Courts Press, 2002)

The Prince of Wales & the Curragh Wren

Greenwood, James, *The Wren of the Curragh* (London: Tinsley Brothers, 1867)

Spoto, Donald, *The Decline and Fall of the House of Windsor* (London: Simon & Schuster, 1995)

Bloody Balfour's Kindly Deeds

Aalen, H. A., Whelan, Kevin and Stout, Matthew, *Atlas of the Irish Rural Landscape* (Cork: Cork University Press, 2011)

Lee, Joseph, *The Modernisation of Irish Society 1848–1918* (Dublin: Gill & Macmillan, 2008)

Wilkins, Noel, *Humble Works for Humble People: A History of the Fishery Piers of County Galway and North Clare, 1800–1922* (County Kildare: Irish Academic Press, 2017)

Killer Gas in the Great War

Barry, Sebastian, *A Long Long Way* (London:
Faber & Faber, 2005). The events of
Hulluch form the backdrop for one of
the most vivid scenes in Barry's epic novel,
which was shortlisted for the Man Booker
Prize in 2005

Bellingham, Lieutenant Colonel Edward
Henry Charles Patrick, Papers and
War Diaries, National Archives, Kew,
WO 374/5648

Bunbury, Turtle, *The Glorious Madness:*
Tales of the Irish and the Great War (Dublin:
Gill & Macmillan, 2014)

Edmonds, Sir James Edward, *Military*
Operations: France and Belgium, 1916:
Volume 1, Sir Douglas Haig's Command to
the 1st July: Battle of the Somme (London:
Macmillan, 1932)

Hope, Carole, *Worshipper and Worshipped:*
Across the Divide – An Irish Padre of the
Great War Fr Willie Doyle, Chaplain to the
Forces, 1915–1917 (Brighton: Reveille
Press, 2013)

Hughes, Gavin, *Fighting Irish: The*
Irish Regiments in the First World War
(County Kildare: Irish Academic
Press, 2015)

Kinsella, Ken, *Out of the Dark 1914–1918:*
South Dubliners Who Fell in the Great
War (County Kildare: Irish Academic
Press, 2014)

McGreevy, Ronan, *Wherever the Firing*
Line Extends: Ireland and the Western
Front (Dublin: The History Press
Ireland, 2016)

See also the Irish Jesuit Archives
(www.jesuitarchives.ie)

Operation Shamrock

Remmel, Herbert, *From Cologne to*
Ballinlough (County Cork: Aubane
Historical Society, 2009)

Acknowledgments

A massive thanks to my ever-astute agent Emma Parry, to Ben Hayes for his timely words of wisdom and to Jo Murray for her diligent scrutiny of matters grammatical, mathematical and otherwise. Thanks also to Isabella Rose Nolan, Jessica Slingsby, Arthur Johnson, Alice Boyle, Charlie Raben, John Onions, Will Fennell, Rory Everard and Alastair Hubert Bao Butler Crampton for helping me to keep my eye on the ball. And to Ally, Jemima and Bay Bunbury, the constant lights of my life.

I have consulted so many kind souls for advice on these chapters and I offer my most hearty thanks for assistance great and small to the following:

Fiona Meade and Dr Kirstin Lemon for putting the magma into my volcano. Dr Marion Dowd and Prof. John Waddell for educating me on very old bears. Martin Kelly (martinjkellytours.com), Declan Moore (Moore Group), Dr Stephen Davis, Cóilín Ó Drisceoil (Kilkenny Archaeology), Stanton Green, James Dempsey (megalithicireland.com), J. S. Dunn, Dan Bradley, Edward Byrne, James Grogan, Cathy Goss, Peter Rochford and Alan O'Neill (Carlow Weather) for guidance on megaliths, eye colours and ancient gold. Leinster rugby legends Rob Kearney and Mike Ross for weighing in with just how many tonnes a scrum could push.

Aidan Walsh, Tim Coughlan, Manchan Magan, Margaret Keane, John Waddell, Mark Clinton, Tony Lowes, Ian Lumley, Úna D'Arcy, Andrew Duncan, Margaret Keane, Ella McSweeney, Paddy Corrigan (Castlepollard Folk Museum), Shirley Clerkin and Caimin O'Brien for their collective insights into the mystery of the togher. Colm Moriarty, Adam Green, Victoria House and Seán Duffy for top tips on the dastardly Vikings. Peter Harbison, Patrick Wallace, Brian Tyrrell, Mairéad Rohan, Dearbhala Ledwidge, Jacqui Doyle, Siobhan Geoghegan and Harry Everard for opening my eyes to the lovely Lingaun.

James O'Higgins Norman, Gearóid Ó Branagáin and Chris McQuinn for helping me to spot wells. Dan Jones, Mathew Forde and Alan Ryan for helping me visualize the Knights Templar. John Kirwan, for his constant guidance on the Butlers. Seamus Bellew, Brendan Mathews and Noel Ross (Co. Louth Archaeological Society) for rewiring my thoughts on Edward the Bruce. Michael Purcell, Dr Margaret Murphy, Dermot Mulligan, Tom La Porte, Elaine Callinan, Michael Brennan, Eileen O'Rourke, Paul Horan and all at Carlow Rootsweb for thoughts great and small on Carlow Castle. Johnny Molloy, Frank Molloy and Caimin O'Brien for leading me into Firceall.

Sarah McHugh, Vicky Herbert, John Patterson, Raphael Mullally and the Maguires of Charlotte, North Carolina, for putting the Maguire story my way. John Cooper and Jane Ohlmeyer for their wily eye on Sir William Stanley. Finola O'Kane and Jay Krehbiel for Lixnaw. Fanchea Gibson and Lady Moyola for Joshua Dawson, and Jessica Rathdonnell, Linda Maher and Manon Somerville for the Byerley Turk. Katarzyna Gmerek, Edward Byrne, Susie Warren and Daniel

Byrne-Rothwell for Tailor Byrne. David Ryan, Morgan J. McCreadie, Rebecca Hayes, David Robinson and Charles Horton for Lord Rosse. William Laffan, Peter Somerville-Large, James Howley, James Peil, Alison Rosse, Regina Lavelle, the Offaly Historical & Archaeological Society and David Ryan for the Hell-Fire Club. David Cotter, Mary Mulhall, Martin Kelly, Finola O'Kane and Nicki Matthews for the Lucan Spa.

David Murphy, Mervyn Greene, Grace Ries, Mette Boye, Howard R. Clarke, Art Cockerill, Peter Goble, John Christopher Farrell, Ronan O Domhnaill, Sammy Leslie, Paul Groff and Brian Nolan for Crimean counsel. Jean Donnelly, Selene Muldowney and Michele Savage for Nellie Clifden. Sé Merry Doyle, Dr Patrick Wallace, Dr Paula Murphy, Jason Ellis, Ronan Sheehan and Mary Heffernan for saluting John Henry Foley. Dr Myles Campbell for his steer on a Chief Secretary's salary. Philip Lecane, Myles Dungan, Ronan McGreevy and Joe Gleeson for the gas attack at Hulluch. Herbert Remmel, Jack Lane, Philip O'Connor, Hugh Glynn, Eileen Courtney, Manus O'Riordan, Ros Dee, Jackie Greene and Stanley Ridgeway for Operation Shamrock.

Index

For Peter Somerville-Large and Charlie Shiffner,
two venerable historical souls who unknowingly
triggered my insatiable thirst to remember.

First published in 2020 in the United States of America by Thames & Hudson
Inc., 500 Fifth Avenue, New York, New York 10110

Library of Congress Control Number 2019940748

www.thamesandhudsonusa.com

ISBN 978-0-500-02253-5

Printed and bound in China by Shanghai Offset Printing Products Limited